THE BOKARO STEEL PLANT
A Study of Soviet Economic Assistance

The Bokaro Steel Plant

A Study of Soviet Economic Assistance

Padma Desai

Research Associate, Russian Research Center, Harvard University

1972

AMERICAN ELSEVIER PUBLISHING COMPANY INC., NEW YORK

North-Holland ISBN: 0 7204 3065 8
American Elsevier ISBN: 0 444 103880

Publishers:

NORTH-HOLLAND PUBLISHING COMPANY – AMSTERDAM
NORTH-HOLLAND PUBLISHING COMPANY, LTD – LONDON

Sole distributors for the U.S.A. and Canada:

AMERICAN ELSEVIER PUBLISHING COMPANY, INC.
52 VANDERBILT AVENUE, NEW YORK, N.Y. 10017

PRINTED IN THE NETHERLANDS

For Ba and Bapuji

Preface

The political economy of steel in India is of interest to all students of underdeveloped countries. They have shaken themselves out of the pre-war myopia of not seeing the wood for the trees and try now to overcome their ignorance of the trees. What is to be done vitally depends on how it is done. Padma Desai's study tells us not only about the anatomy but also about the physiology of development, not only about its economics but also about its politics. One can learn from errors in economics; they are easily detected. Irrationalities on the other hand abound in every country's politics. This study offers a rational analysis of the partly irrational "much heat and little light" of Indian debates about steel.

"Steel mills should be in the public not the private sector" became part of Indian ideology in the 1950's but opposite theoretical arguments about Indian steel mills arose in the United States. While the original decision on public investment in steel was functional — the private sector was neither willing nor capable of mobilizing enough capital or of assuming such risks in the immediate post-war period — theology only took over in the 1950's.

Nor was the U.S.S.R. decision not to cooperate with the Indian private consultant firm of Dastur & Co. but to build the Bokaro steel mill as a "turn-key project" predominantly due to ideological reluctance to work with "the private sector". It was probably largely due to a preference for relying on one's known resources without the complication and risks of partnership.

Padma Desai's account of the emotionally loaded debate is admirably lucid and is — as the author rightly claims — "sufficiently anti-American, anti-Soviet, anti-Dastur, and anti-Indian bureaucracy to be completely objective".

Not only politics but also the economics of steel are complex. India ought to have a comparative advantage in steel. It has the raw materials (iron, ore, and coking coal) the human resources and a market with sufficient effective demand. In a free trade world India should export steel to and import wheat from the U.S. Yet Indian costs and prices of steel are still, after two decades of industrialization, higher than those of Europe or Japan. These may be infant industry troubles. Learning on the job and learning from experience both to run and to plan steel mills should lower costs in the longer run. Australia and South Africa built up a steel industry in the 1930s under what looked then to be a comparative cost disadvantage. After a generation — but not sooner — they are today among the most efficient steel producers. The infant industry gestation period seems to extend to two or three decades, not to two or three five-year plans.

Will costs of steel in India fall in time? Let us remember that investment costs per ton of steel capacity are higher for a two million ton steel mill, when that mill is to grow to four or five million ton capacity, than for one which is to remain at a two million ton output. The author gives the cost estimates of different comparable steel mills in the world economy and distinguishes between short run, below full capacity and long run, full capacity costs. Owing to the higher prices of local building materials and machinery Indian costs are still higher than those of efficient steel-producing countries. In the long run however the costs of input may also fall. Increasing returns may materialize in three sectors: in steel production, in the development of national steel planning technology, and in construction and equipment costs. These costs moreover have to be calculated at shadow prices. National steel production undoubtedly substitutes imports. Producing bananas on the North Pole is also an import substitution. How high a price should one be willing to pay for import substitution? What progress in costs reduction has been achieved on other Indian steel mills? Those are the problems the author examines. The full evidence from the record of the last fifteen years is not yet available and the time period is still too short for it to be fully conclusive. Such evidence as is available, however, is admirably presented. It is too early for conclusive answers, but the relevant questions are asked. Stating a problem correctly is usually more than half the answer. When full evidence shall become available a definite judgment on Indian steel production may be made. The present work will be one of the most important stepping stones to a definitive study; no researcher can afford to overlook it.

P.N. Rosenstein-Rodan

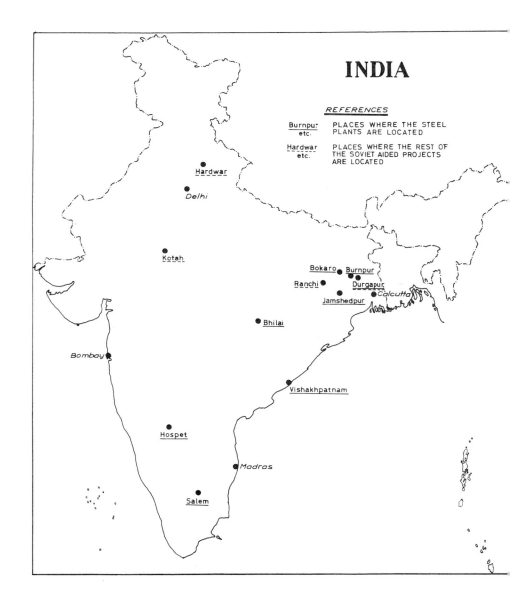

INDIA

REFERENCES

Burnpur
etc.

PLACES WHERE THE STEEL
PLANTS ARE LOCATED

Hardwar
etc.

PLACES WHERE THE REST OF
THE SOVIET AIDED PROJECTS
ARE LOCATED

Hardwar

Delhi

Kotah

Bokaro Burnpur
Ranchi Durgapur
Jamshedpur Calcutta

Bhilai

Bombay

Vishakhpatnam

Hospet

Madras

Salem

Author's preface

The Bokaro steel plant in India and the Aswan dam in Egypt are unique in the history of U.S.-Soviet aid rivalry: in each case, the U.S. came to be identified with a massive project of national importance, opted out conspicuously and the Soviet Union stepped in.

But the parallels end there. The Soviet Union has traditionally managed to secure generous returns on its aid program in India by "doing what the West would not do", especially in the areas of heavy industry and oil. However, in the case of the Bokaro steel plant, it landed itself into a tricky and novel situation. By the time aid negotiations for the steel plant were initiated, India had already reached a stage of technological maturity so that local expertise in designing and constructing steel plants was available. Indeed, the prestigious Indian firm of M.N. Dastur and Company was actively associated with the early planning of the project and had the competence to assess criticially the proposed Soviet designs; it was, however, muscled out by the Soviet negotiators from the final aid-contract to the chagrin of an articulate and aroused public opinion cutting across most political parties.

The complex and fascinating series of events, originating

with the initial planning of Bokaro and culminating in the Soviet "takeover" of the project and the controversies surrounding the outcome, form the subject matter of this long essay. It should be of interest to the students of aid diplomacy and the aid process. It illustrates pointedly the limitations imposed by the aid-tying practices of donor countries on the transfer of advanced technologies to the developing countries. Above all, it is of direct relevance to the future course of Soviet economic assistance to, and influence in, India.

In the course of tracing the history of events constituting this essay, I have incurred the debt of numerous officials and friends. P.K. Basu, M.V. Desai, J. Luther and H.Y. Sharda Prasad were particularly helpful. T.N. Srinivasan and A. Vaidyanathan provided detailed comments on an earlier draft. The incisive comments of S. Guhan at each stage of completing the essay have imparted not only a blow-by-blow quality to the narration but also a sharp focus on the policy issues. However, I alone remain responsible for the errors and the judgments, especially on the analytical issues.

I have also benefited from seminars based on this essay at the Development Advisory Service and the Russian Research Center, both at Harvard University, and at Cornell University. I am particularly grateful to Abram Bergson and Richard Eckaus for detailed comments and useful discussions on an earlier draft and to Joseph Berliner for drawing my attention to the Survey prepared by the Organisation for Economic Co-operation and Development on the continuous casting of steel in the Soviet Union.

The research on this essay was financed by the M.I.T. Center for International Studies where I was a DSR Staff Member for three years beginning from July 1968. The facilities of the Russian Research Center at Harvard University where I have been a Research Associate since July 1968 have made the task of working on this essay immensely agreeable. I would particularly like to record my gratitude to Max Millikan, the late Director of the M.I.T. Center, for his constant interest and encouragement. I am also grateful to Paul Rosenstein-Rodan for having written a special preface to the essay and for having given me the benefit, through numerous discussions, of his vast experience and insights into the problems of aid and technology transfers.

The map of India showing the locations of the various projects cited in the essay was prepared at the Cartographic Section of the Indian Statistical Institute at New Delhi. The successive manuscripts were typed with good cheer by S. Rangarajan of the India International Center at New Delhi and Eileen Smith at the M.I.T. Center for International Studies. Patricia Grady edited the manuscript with patience and skill. The task of finalising the manuscript was considerably expedited by the sustained interest of Amy Leiss.

The first draft of this essay was completed during a two-week stay at Poona. The organisation of the material and the writing was eased beyond measure by the cheerful co-operation and the warmth of Hansa, Vidyut, Mona, Vijay, Sukumar and Manoj.

Cambridge, Massachusetts   *Padma Desai*
September 1971

Glossary of
Indian terms and units

Indian units
1 crore: 10 million
1 lakh: 100,000

Political institutions and parties

Lok Sabha: Lower House of the Indian Parliament

Rajya Sabha: Upper House of the Indian Parliament

Committee on Public Undertakings of the Lok Sabha: These committees of the Lok Sabha consisting of members of various political parties review from time to time the performance of the various undertakings of the Government of India. Their reports are supposed to be objective and critical in their evaluation of the subject under consideration.

Estimates Committee of the Lok Sabha: These committees generally undertake an evaluation of the various ministries and departments of the Government of India. In practice, the reports of both these sets of committees promote the accountability of the Executive branch of the Government to the Parliament.

Communist Party of India (CPI):   The Moscow-oriented Indian communist party.

Communist Party — Marxist (CPM):   The CPM was formed after the Chinese invasion of 1962. Its orientation is neither Soviet nor Chinese.

Communist Party — Marxist-Leninist (CPML):   The CPML is militant in its ideology and violent in its tactics. It is most active in West Bengal, especially in Calcutta city. It is Mao-inspired.

Congress Party (Ruling):   The faction of the old Congress Party, with a left of center program, which was swept to power under Mrs. Gandhi's leadership after the General Elections of March 1971.

Congress Party (Organizational):   The faction of the old Congress Party with an old, conservative leadership.

Dravid Munnetra Kazhagam (DMK):   The political party with a regional basis in the state of Tamil Nadu in South India with Madras as the capital.

Jan Sangh: The right wing party drawing its inspiration from Hindu cultural traditions and nationalist aspirations.

Praja Socialist Party (PSP):   The socialist impact of this party, formed in 1952, was nullified mainly as a result of the socialist program of the Congress Party under Nehru's leadership.

Swatantra Party: The right wing party of private enterprise.

Samyukta Socialist Party (SSP):   The socialist party under the colorful leadership of the late Ram Manohar Lohia with a strictly agitational approach.

Soviet-aided projects cited in the study

Heavy Engineering Corporation (HEC) at Ranchi in Bihar State in Eastern India; it manufactures steel plant machinery.

Heavy Electrical Equipment Plant (HEEP) at Hardwar in the State of Uttar Pradesh in Northern India.

Kotah Instrumentation Project at Kotah in Rajasthan State in North-Western India; it manufactures precision instruments for the requirements of heavy industry.

Mining and Allied Machinery Corporation (MAMC) at Durgapur in the State of West Bengal in Eastern India.

Steel plants cited in the study

Public sector steel plants:

Bhilai: It is situated in the State of Madhya Pradesh in Central India. It is Soviet-collaborated and its current capacity is rated at 2.5 million tonnes of ingot steel per annum. It produces billets, rails, sleeper bars, structurals and rods.

Durgapur: It is situated in the State of West Bengal in Eastern India. It is British-collaborated and its current capacity is rated at 1.6 million tonnes of ingot steel per annum. It produces blooms, billets, sheets and axles.

Rourkela: It is situated in Orissa State in Eastern India. It is German-collaborated and its current capacity is rated at 1.8 million tonnes of ingot steel per annum. It specializes in flat products.

Private sector steel plants:

Tata Iron and Steel Company (TISCO):   It is situated in Jamshedpur in Bihar State in Eastern India. It produces a variety of items and its current capacity is rated at 2 million tonnes of ingot steel per annum.

Indian Iron and Steel Company (IISCO):   It is situated in Burnpur in the State of West Bengal in Eastern India. Its current capacity is rated at 1 million tonnes of ingot steel per annum.

Abbreviations

BSL: Bokaro Steel Limited. It was formed as an Indian Government Company in 1964 and entrusted with the task of setting up the Bokaro Steel Plant and of developing ancillary facilities such as the township and sources of supply of raw materials.

CEDB: Central Engineering and Design Bureau. It is an Indian Government Company which prepares project reports on steel plants and designs steel plant equipment.

Dasturco: The Indian firm of consulting engineers of M.N. Dastur and Company.

HSCL: Hindustan Steel Construction Limited. It was formed in 1967 as an Indian Government Company for the purpose of undertaking the construction work on the Bokaro Steel Plant.

HSL: Hindustan Steel Limited. It was set up in 1955 as an Indian Government Company and entrusted with the management of the three steel plants in the public sector.

Gipromez: The Soviet Design Institute for steel plants.

Tiazpromexport: The Soviet State Agency for exports.

U.S. AID: United States Agency for International Development.

Contents

CHAPTER 1

Introduction

The Bokaro Steel Plant is currently under construction in the Eastern region of India with Soviet assistance. It is designed to roll out flat products and its first stage of 1.7 million tonnes[1] of ingot steel is expected to be commissioned in June 1973.

Bokaro is the fourth steel plant in the Indian public sector and the second, after Bhilai, to be constructed with Soviet aid. As is well known, Soviet aid participation in India, which began in 1955, has grown steadily over the years. Indeed most analysts of Soviet aid to India maintain that the 'returns' to the Soviet Union have been far out of proportion to the actual magnitude of its aid to India because the Soviet Union has concentrated on 'impact type' projects; further that these are projects which the West, especially the United States, was not interested in promoting or which, having considered for aid, it eventually chose to turn down.

It would seem that the Bokaro Steel Plant fits this description perfectly. It is a massive project, which, when completed to its eventual capacity of 5.5 million tonnes of ingot steel, will be one of the largest integrated steelworks anywhere. It is also a project for which American aid did

1

not come through. And yet, if the sustained controversies in the Indian parliament and the press are any indication, the 'returns' to the Soviet Union from Bokaro are unlikely to match those arising from Bhilai or from its aid offensive in the Indian oil industry.

The major purpose of the study, therefore, is to narrate and analyse in depth the series of events in the continuing history of the steel plant which have contributed to such a possibility. It covers all the details from the Indian Planning Commission's initial conception to the current controversies surrounding it more than a decade later. The treatment of the theme is both chronological and analytical and the major episodes in the history over a period of fifteen years are documented and analyzed at length.

It is particularly emphasized that the evolution of the main features of the steel plant over time and their final shape with Soviet collaboration resulted from the continuous interaction of three major elements with the initial conception of the steel plant. These three elements are: (1) the problems arising from the need for foreign collaboration for the project; (2) the availability in India of the prestigious firm of consulting engineers, M.N. Dastur and Company, who were originally intended to play a dominating role in designing and building the steel plant; and (3) the policy objectives relating to the steel industry in India. The decisions about the location of the project and the type of products it should manufacture were relevant but not critical to this interaction process; hence, they are dealt with briefly in the next section.

The details of the original (Indian Planning Commission) scheme of Bokaro which envisaged an initial capacity of one million tons of steel ingots with the possibility of expansion to ten million tons, and Dastur and Company as designers and builders, are presented in Chapter 3. It is particularly stressed that this scheme carried a built-in potential for confrontations later on at various levels. First, only minimal imports of equipment and services of steel technologists were planned and it was hoped that these would be financed with American aid. In other words, the expectation was that the foreign supplier of aid-financed equipment and services would settle for a marginal role in a project as massive and prestigious as Bokaro. Second, no alternative source of foreign finance, in case American aid for a public sector steel plant in India did not materialize, was indicated. Finally, the dominating role assigned to a private sector consulting firm in designing and building a public sector steel plant was also to prove critical.

The problems and implications of securing foreign aid for the project are discussed in Chapters 4 and 5. In Chapter 4 the reasons for the failure of American aid to materialize for this project — an aid which had been advocated and advanced with considerable energy and commitment by the liberal leadership of Galbraith and Kennedy — are traced to ideological considerations and the economic interests of the U.S. steel and shipping lobbies.

The chronology of events resulting in an agreement with the Soviet Union is narrated in Chapter 5. Two aspects are stressed. In the first place, Indian bargaining strength was severely constrained from the very beginning by the total absence of an alternative offer of aid-financed equipment for the plant and by the unwillingness of the Government of India to finance the import requirements through free foreign exchange. Therefore, the initial concession led to many more. Second, the eventual course of negotiations, the features of the collaboration agreement with the Soviet Union, and, gradually, of the project itself were crucially influenced by the emergence of a rapport between the two countries on certain policy objectives relating to the development of the steel industry in India.

These policy objectives are also analyzed in Chapter 5. Thus, the decision to expand the steel industry in the Indian *public sector* appears to have been extended also to the setting up of the required designing, engineering, and construction services in the public sector. The second policy objective, which pervades the entire growth process in India, is *import substitution*. The Soviet Union was willing to cooperate on both these objectives, as they coincided with her own approach to these questions. Indeed, the Indian predilection for using Indian products by utilizing the capacities of several public sector projects designed to supply the requirements of steel plant construction coincided with the Soviet objective of their efficient utilization as these projects are all Soviet-financed. At the same time, the adverse publicity and reaction in India which followed from the Soviet insistence on downgrading the Indian firm, Dastur and Company, appear to have prompted both the Soviet Union and the Indian government to place greater emphasis on associating and developing Indian *public sector* knowhow in steel-plant construction and providing for its utilization in the *expansion* phase of the Bokaro plant.

One important episode in this process of interaction and of the negotiations with the Soviet Union was the detailed Cost Reduction Study prepared by Dastur and Company at the request of the Indian Steel Ministry, with a view to suggesting cost reductions in the Soviet Project Report for Bokaro. These proposals are discussed separately in Chapter 6. In particular, the analysis seeks to answer specific questions such as whether an inferior technology was being provided by the Soviet Union for Bokaro. The controversy on this issue exemplifies the problems likely to be encountered increasingly by donor countries in tying sales of technologies with aid to developing countries where local expertise capable of judging these technologies exists.

In Chapter 7 the current controversies on Bokaro are discussed in relation to relevant detailed factual evidence. In general, these controversies appear to be biased and to generate more heat than light.

Finally, the details of the story are narrated. It bears

some resemblance to a Greek tragedy, insofar as the original proposal for Bokaro contained elements that were to create controversies and conflicts if the project was to materialize. The analysis has important implications for the future expansion of the Indian steel industry, the efficiency of the donor-recipient relationship, and the future possibility of the Soviet Union reaping the kind of spectacular political benefits which it had traditionally derived (e.g., in oil refining and prospecting) by 'doing things which the West would not'. These issues are discussed in Chapter 8.

It is hoped that, in a debate currently charged with emotion, the narrative and analysis will be found sufficiently anti-American, anti-Soviet, anti-Dastur, and anti-Indian-bureaucracy to be considered completely objective.

Note to Chapter 1

[1] One ton is equivalent to 1.096 (metric) tonnes. The American sources referred to in the text employ the measure of ton and the Soviet sources, of tonne. With the introduction of the metric system in India, the Indian sources switched to the use of tonne in the sixties. However, the difference between the two measures is insignificant, and the Indian sources seem to use them interchangeably.

CHAPTER 2

The location and size of Bokaro

The Bokaro Steel Plant did not have a smooth beginning with respect to its location. Of the various sites[1] considered by the Colombo Plan Mission in 1955, that ultimately selected for the plant was rejected by the Mission 'because it was the remotest from existing means of communication'.[2] However,

> ... having chosen Durgapur as the site for the third steelworks, Government decided in September 1955 to develop the eastern site at Bokaro[3] which but for difficulties in communication, afforded excellent facilities that could be taken advantage of for the location of *any* steel plant that might be set up at a later stage. The Ministry of Iron & Steel, therefore, proposed a provision of Rs. 3.75 crores in the Second Five Year Plan to develop the Bokaro area, including a railway bridge across the river Damodar at Bokaro and adequate road communication.[4]

Thus, it would seem that around 1955 extensive rail and road construction for the location of a steel plant was begun in the 'Bokaro area'. The decision to locate the plant in Maraphari village (now Bokaro Steel City), 310 kilometers southwest of Calcutta in the Hazaribagh district of Bihar, was made in 1957.[5]

However, it would be misleading to conclude that considerations arising exclusively from raw material endowments[6] had a painless fruition in the choice of the site at Bokaro Steel City. Regionalism, which is generally at play in the decisions to locate industrial capacities in India, is most assertive in the case of steel.[7]

In the first place, the raw materials required for a steel plant are sufficiently well-scattered in the eastern, central, and to some extent the southern regions of the country for a case to be made out for a steel plant in about half a dozen places. The most persistent claimants have been Goa on the West Coast, Hospet in Mysore, Salem in Tamil Nadu, and Visakhapatnam in Andhra Pradesh. Moreover, the choice was complicated further by divergence of opinion among special committees assigned this task. Thus, it was reported that while the British American Steelworks for India Consortium (BASIC) had recommended Visakhapatnam over Hospet and Salem as the site for the fifth steel plant, Dastur & Company,[8] as well as other technical committees of the Government of India, had favored Salem.[9] Second, with increasing political decentralization, the aspirant state often sought to dismiss any inadequacies in the site of a potential steel plant with arguments such as Japan producing cheap steel without any domestic resources! Finally, the sheer size of Bokaro, as its planning gradually evolved, provided the regional aspirants with ammunition for arguments in favor of more dispersed steel capacities, and even of diverting the resources proposed for Bokaro to alternative uses such as fertilizers.

Thus, the memorandum prepared by the Salem Steel Plant Committee in 1966 suggested establishing at Visakhapatnam, Hospet, and Salem steel plants each with a capacity of 500,000 tonnes of ingot, at a total cost of Rs. 450 crores. It was estimated that Rs. 300 crores could be released by limiting Bokaro's capacity to one million tonnes and providing facilities for future expansion to two million tonnes. The remaining Rs. 150 crores could be found by reducing expenditures on the development of transport facilities in the steel belt in the eastern region. The argument was further buttressed by the suggestion that this alternative policy of 'medium sized' plants would result in the speedy completion of all the projects.[10] At a public meeting on July 24, 1967, the Tamil Nadu Chief Minister, Mr. C.N. Annadurai, called for diverting the funds allotted to Bokaro in order to set up three 'small' steel plants, one each at Hospet, Salem, and Visakhapatnam.[11] The regional claim was advanced from a slightly different perspective by the Tamil Nadu Industries Minister, Mr. R. Venkatraman, when he observed that the cost, estimated at Rs. 35 crores, of the water supply and drainage system alone of the Bokaro steel plant (presumably for its first stage of 1.7 million tonnes) '(would) suffice to finance the Salem Steel Plant in the first stage'.[12] These details are presented with a view to emphasizing that the Bokaro Steel Plant *did* in fact survive the pressures generated by the 'politics of steel' to become the fourth public-sector steel plant at Bokaro Steel City. Both its scheduling and scale were, however, to be affected by rival claims to the limited resources available for steel plants.[13]

Along with the decision on location, the decision to manufacture *flat products* at Bokaro became crystallized around the beginning of the Second Five Year Plan in April, 1956. Besides the advantages arising from resource endowments, a powerful motivation for setting up steel capacities is the Indian desire to 'save foreign exchange' spent on imported steel. As early as the Second Five Year Plan, the gap between domestic requirements and domestic production was becoming pronounced in all categories of steel, especially in the category of flat steel products. It was clear that as industrial development accelerated and became more diversified, the demand for flat products was likely to increase at a faster rate than that for structurals, bars, and rods.[14] Thus, preparations for the Second Five

Year Plan indicated that flat product capacities in addition to the one planned for Rourkela were necessary.[15] Thus, in 1957 HSL assigned to Dasturco the preparation of a Preliminary Project Report for an integrated steel plant in Bokaro Steel City which was specifically to manufacture flat products.

Notes to Chapter 2

[1] These were in the eastern part of the country. Two were near Sindri in West Bengal, two near Bokaro Steel City in Bihar, and one at Durgapur in West Bengal. See the *68th Report of the Committee on Public Undertakings (1969-70) of the Fourth Lok Sabha*, entitled *Bokaro Steel Ltd.*, (New Delhi: Lok Sabha Secretariat, April 1970), p. 10. (Hereafter referred to as the *68th Report*.)

[2] Ibid., p. 1.

[3] This phrasing in the *68th Report* seems to imply that the Government, having acted upon one suggestion of the Colombo Plan Mission by selecting Durgapur as the site for the third steel plant, decided to overrule the Mission's negative suggestion with respect to the site at Bokaro.

[4] Ibid., p. 1 (my italics).

[5] The *68th Report* states rather vividly: 'The Bokaro Steel Plant was conceived in 1957 when the Government asked Hindustan Steel Ltd. to take preliminary steps for the installation of the new steelworks at Bokaro', p. 75. Hindustan Steel Ltd. (HSL) was set up in 1955 as a Government of India company and entrusted with the management of the three steel plants in the Indian public sector.

[6] The fact that the Heavy Engineering Corporation (HEC), the major Indian supplier of equipment for Bokaro, was also located in Bihar probably influenced the choice of site for the steel plant in Bihar. On the other hand, the Planning Commission Note on Bokaro, *which came later*, makes no reference to the possibility of HEC supplying equipment for Bokaro.

[7] For an extensive discussion of regional influence in the location of Indian industry during 1950-1966, see J. Bhagwati and Padma Desai, *Planning for Industralization: A Study of India's Trade and Industrial Policies Since 1950*, O.E.C.D. Development Center (London: Oxford University Press, 1970).

[8] The name and fortunes of this private sector consulting firm (hereafter referred to as Dasturco) continue to be embroiled, to this

date, in the controversies surrounding Bokaro and, indeed, the Indian steel industry. The *68th Report* of the C.P.U. contains details of Dr. Dastur's initiation to the Indian steel scene. When in India in 1954 as an American citizen and as a TCM consultant on an American mission for the expansion program of Mysore Iron and Steel Company, he was 'inspired' by T. T. Krishnamachari, then Minister of Commerce and Industry, to set up the consulting firm. In the next three years, 'the company succesfully handled various projects in the private sector such as a ferro-manganese plant for Tatas secured against severe international competition and completed eight months ahead of schedule. However, the Company did not receive any work on the steel programme initiated by Government in the Second Five Year Plan.' (*68th Report*, p. 9.) As the only Indian consulting organization of repute on steel plants, Dasturco was asked in October 1958 to prepare a Preliminary Project Report for Bokaro.

[9] *The Patriot* (New Delhi), November 4, 1968.

[10] *The Hindu* (Madras), November 27, 1966.

[11] *The Hindu* (Madras), July 25, 1967.

[12] For a plant size of 500,000 tonnes at Salem, this rhetoric would yield a plant investment cost per tonne of Rs. 700 which is lower than the comparable figures of Rs. 992 for the Fukuyama plant in Japan and Rs. 861 for the Taranto plant in Italy.

[13] The resource position was further strained by two successive harvest failures in 1966 and 1967. These affected not only the generation of resources in the system but also necessitated their diversion for purposes of drought relief. Incidentally, the fact that the massive expense on Bokaro would be phased out over a period of a decade and hence would make its absorption more feasible than if the same scale of expenditure were pumped into the system simultaneously over three steel plants was lost sight of by the different regional claimants.

[14] It is not clear if the sequencing of steel capacities and their product-mix corresponded strictly to the unfolding pattern of demand. In general, the momentum was provided by the decision to produce more steel. The three steel plants in the public sector, each specializing broadly in a given category of items, were initiated almost simultaneously. Thus, the project report for the 1 million tonne capacity of the Rourkela Steel Plant, specializing in flat products, was submitted in November 1955 and its 1 million tonne capacity fully commissioned in 1962. The project report for the Bhilai Steel Plant, specializing in billets, rails, sleepers bars, structurals, and rods, with its 1 million tonne capacity, was submitted in December 1955 and its capacity fully commissioned in January 1961. The project report for the Durgapur Steel Plant, specializing in

blooms, billets, sheets, and axles, was submitted in 1956 and its one million tonne capacity fully commissioned in 1962.

[15] It should, however, be emphasized that while there was recognition of shortage in flat steel items and that while detailed estimates of requirements were prepared from time to time by the Perspective Planning Division of the Indian Planning Commission, the decisions relating to the scheduling of Bokaro capacities seem to have been only partially governed by calculations of requirements. For a further discussion of this point, see footnote 10, p. 49.

CHAPTER 3

The original conception of Bokaro

The details of the original conception and implementation of Bokaro are set forth in a Note entitled 'Bokaro Steel Project — Problems of Implementation', prepared by the Indian Planning Commission around 1961.[1] These details pertain to (a) the aims to be fulfilled by the project and (b) the arrangements spelled out for implementing them. The arrangements can be grouped further into (1) the provision of consulting services for the project, including its designing and engineering and supervision of its construction; (2) provisions for foreign collaboration on the project, and (3) the organizational and procedural arrangements necessary for the speedy implementation of the project.

A. The Aims of the Bokaro Project

The aims of Bokaro, as stated in the Note, were majestic. They reemphasized the planning strategy, initiated by the Second Five Year Plan in 1956 — namely, that of linking the destiny of Indian economic development to the growth of the steel industry. Indeed, the Bokaro objectives went beyond the goal of economic salvation through steel. The note expressed the optimistic view that, after the experience gained from setting up three steel plants with extensive foreign collaboration, India had acquired enough expertise in steel technology to design a *Swadeshi* (indigenous) steel plant. Even the capacity for fabricating heavy machinery and structurals was considered broad-based enough to make the import requirements of these items for Bokaro marginal. Again, the immediate objective of 'expeditiously' reaching an initial capacity of one million ingot tons per year reflected a similar determination to achieve self-reliance by gradually reducing imports of flat steel items. This objective also aimed at emphasizing, in terms of a reduced gestation period, that Bokaro's capacities would be activated according to a decisive time schedule. Bokaro represented a challenge and an exercise in self-assertion.

The specific aims of Bokaro were stated as follows:

> The Bokaro plant as now planned will have initial capacity of one million ingot tons per annum (to be completed by 1965/66), capable of rapid expansion to 3-4 million tons, with provision for future expansion when required to about 10 million tons. Current plans provide for expansion of Bokaro to over 3 million tons' production by 1970.[2]

Thus, the massive size envisioned in the original scheme gave Bokaro a prestige. A little later, it was also mentioned specifically that the plant must be constructed 'most efficiently and expeditiously'.[3]

It was, however, the indirect, long-term objectives that gave Bokaro its grandeur. These transcended the immediate task of turning out flat steel products. Setting up the plant was to provide 'maximum opportunity for Indian engineering talent' and use 'indigenous equipment to the fullest extent' so that 'further industrial development of the country is stimulated'.

B. Implementing the Objectives of Bokaro
These arrangements were specified in provisions for consul-

ting services, foreign collaboration, and managing the implementation of the project. The consulting firm of M.N. Dastur & Company was to continue to assist the Indian Planning Commission and Hindustan Steel Ltd., as they had been doing since 1959.[4]

The Note was brief and guarded on the provision of foreign collaboration for Bokaro. 'It is understood that there is [a] good prospect that foreign exchange for the project may come from the United States through AID, the new agency.[5]

The organizational and procedural modifications necessary for the speedy implementation of Bokaro were based on the realization that HSL, the currently existing agency for managing public-sector steel plants, would not be able to undertake full responsibility for the implementation of the Bokaro project.

Therefore it was explicitly stated that 'the overall design and engineering of the plant would be done by Dastur and Company, the Consulting Engineers. The report, plant layout and detailed specifications would be reviewed by a U.S. steel producer to act as 'Production Adviser',[6] and the task of managing the construction of the plant would be entrusted to a separate organization.

Consulting Services: From the preparation of the Project Report to the management of the construction of the project, the Note explicitly specified a dominating role for Dasturco. (Indeed this was its most striking feature.) In addition to the Detailed Project Report for Bokaro and the specifications for equipment and structurals, Dasturco was to prepare the manning lists, job specifications, recruitment schedule, training programs, and the required syllabi and manuals. Afterwards, it was to handle all procedural requirements connected with these details, i.e., issuing the inquiries for equipment and structurals on behalf of HSL, receiving and scrutinizing the equipment tenders, and recommending suppliers with a view to 'the maximum utilization of Indian sources of equipment'.[7] It was also to inspect the equipment and organize and direct the training program.

At the next stage of managing the construction of the plant, Dasturco was to prepare detailed schedules of the construction requirements, including materials and structurals, and the timetable of the entire construction activity, and lay out the procedures for the smooth functioning of the construction operations. In organizing the construction, the firm was to issue tenders in its own name, select competent contractors, and implement the work, providing the normal guarantees and penalties. Dasturco's participation was extended to the setting up of equipment, fabricated structurals and cranes, electrical equipment, and utilities. It was not only to supervise the setting up of indigenous equipment by domestic contractors, but was also to ensure that foreign equipment suppliers utilized Indian labor to the extent stimulated in their contracts.

Foreign Collaboration: Compared to the role of the Indian consultants, that of the foreign collaborators envisaged in the scheme was marginal. The U.S. steel producer (in the capacity of 'Production Adviser') was to scrutinize the Detailed Project Report prepared by Dasturco and point out any deficiencies. It would also suggest improvements in Indian designs and scrutinize the specifications for the equipment and structurals. (These would, however, be put in final form by Dasturco.) The need for foreign technicians was assessed at '30 to 40 top ranking foreign steel plant technicians, from the works of the U.S. 'Production Adviser', to man the key posts at the Bokaro Steel Project for a limited period of time'.[8]

Organizational and Procedural Changes: Several reasons were advanced for HSL's inability to undertake full responsibility for the implementation of Bokaro. In the first place, HSL needed to streamline its organizational structure and its procedures for operating existing steel capacities. Second, it was already loaded down with the task of expanding the capacities of the existing steel plants. Finally, the renovated organizational setup for Bokaro was intended to serve as an ideal in management for future as well as existing, steel plants. Thus, Bokaro would start off with a 'clean slate' not only with regard to its conception as a plant with a built-in potential for expansion up to 10 to 12 million tonnes, 'designed and engineered by an Indian firm of consulting engineers', but also as a model for managing the construction and operating of steel plants in India.[9]

Three arguments were advanced suggesting that this arrangement, in which the foreign collaborator was to play a marginal role, would ensure the fulfillment of the specific objective of the efficient and expeditious completion of the plant. The first argument cited Dasturco's reputation for professional expertise. It was known to employ engineers with fifteen to twenty years' experience in designing and constructing steel plants. The firm had also prepared the Preliminary Report for Bokaro which had not only been thoroughly scrutinized by the Technical Committee of HSL, but had also been commended by the Russian and American steel experts who had seen it.[10]

The second argument was in terms of the checks and balances provided for ensuring the efficient completion of the plant. While the HSL Technical Committee would scrutinize the Detailed Project Report to be prepared by Dasturco, the U.S. 'Production Adviser' was to point out the deficiencies. The equipment suppliers, who were to fabricate the equipment to Dasturco's design and specification, would have to guarantee that it would work satisfactorily. Finally, as an indigenous firm whose reputation and future was staked in India, Dasturco would be compelled to do its best.[11]

The final and most substantial argument in favor of the arrangement followed from the objective that the plant should be designed and constructed to suit Indian conditions for efficient operation.[12] This would apply to the entire construction activity including the design, fabrication, and erection of equipment and structurals. The extent to which the jobs of designing, fabricating, and constructing at each level could be successfully undertaken by indigenous fabricating capacities and by locally available skills was considerable. For example, definite advantages could be expected to accrue from having structural items designed by Indian consultants who were aware of Indian fabricating limitations. Such an arrangement would ensure operational efficiency, speed of execution as also substantial import-substitution (for if the requirements could not be fabricated indigenously, they would have to be imported). As an instance, it was pointed out that Indian fabricators could not manufacture the structurals for the Foundry Forge Plant of HEC at Ranchi, designed by the Czech collaborators; the structurals were more complex than were either 'necessary or desirable' and had to be imported.[13] Again, it was indicated that structurals designed in the United States would be difficult to manufacture in India, simply because the U.S. concept of structural design is different. Morever, the switch to the metric system in India would require massive revision of items designed in the United States. In the management of construction, advantages would also arise from Indian consultants' familiarity with the procedures and practices of Indian contractors setting up the structurals.[14]

There seemed to be no shortage of Indian firms capable of undertaking the entire civil construction work for the plant.[15] The setting up of *indigenous* equipment could be done by Indian firms such as Ramji Dahyawala, who erected the blast furnace at Bhilai. There was also a strong possibility of *imported* equipment being set up with the participation of Indian contractors and labor. This was done by Voest of Austria, who, with the help of Indian contractors and labor, successfully set up the LD steel melting shop at Rourkela.

In contrast to this detailed listing of the possibilities of import-substitution in fabricating and erecting structurals in construction jobs, the Note contained no details on the possibility of utilizing Indian *equipment* for Bokaro. It made no reference at all to the possibility of manufacturing some of the required equipment at the Heavy Machine Building Plant at Ranchi, being set up with Soviet aid. It was hopefully stated that 'intensive efforts should be made to maximize the indigenous content of the project to give impetus to the Indian economic development, which should be one of the basic objects of U.S. aid to India'.[16]

Thus, the Planning Commission based its initial conception of Bokaro on the possibility of American aid, with Dasturco playing the dominant role in designing and constructing the plant.[17] It was hoped that American aid would finance purchases of equipment from U.S. suppliers and the services of a few U.S. steel technicians, whereas practically the entire requirement for structurals and contractors' services would be met from indigenous sources.

The optimism and confidence that pervaded the Note — indeed the entire scheme — were however destined to undergo severe buffeting for a number of reasons. In the first place, the Note was overconfident in presuming that the probability of the U.S. participating in a massive Indian public-sector steel plant would not be zeroed out by possible American unwillingness to undertake any such collaboration.[18]

Furthermore, within India itself, a scheme that envisaged a dominating role for a private-sector consulting firm in a public-sector steel plant was likely to generate ideological confrontation.[19] While the Planning Commission may take a nonideological attitude on such an issue, other elements in the Indian political-economic-bureaucratic complex — the steel ministry, for instance — might have been expected to strive for a preponderant role, extending to provision of consulting services, for the public sector.

Other considerations, essentially motivated by the self-interest of the foreign participant, were likely to affect Bokaro's fortunes. With the increasing tendency toward aid-tying, it was rather unrealistic to assume that aid-financed supplies of equipment would be given by any collaborator without his insisting on doing the consulting too. Such insistence would also arise from the Indian scheme's requirement that the project — at least in its first stage — be completed efficiently and expeditiously; that is, the foreign collaborators, arguing in terms of the risks, delays, and imperfections supposedly endemic to the Indian scene, would not guarantee a time-bound completion unless they were left free to undertake the whole operation themselves. These arguments were likely to be further bolstered by considerations of prestige; collaboration in an Indian steel plant has traditionally been regarded by foreign aid-donors as a matter of staking not only their finances but also the reputation of their technology and expertise and as a politically conspicuous measure of their generosity and efficiency in promoting economic development and industrialization.

It would therefore seem that the fate of the Bokaro steel plant was ill-starred from the beginning.

Notes to Chapter 3

[1] It is hereafter referred to as the 'Planning Commission Note on Bokaro'.

[2] Ibid., p. 2.

[3] Ibid., p. 3.

[4] See 'Planning Commission Note on Bokaro', p. 2. The Note specifically stated: 'The present concept of [the] Bokaro plant is in accordance with the preliminary project report of M. N. Dastur & Company of Calcutta, Consulting Engineers, submitted in December 1959.'

[5] Ibid., p. 2.

[6] Ibid., p. 3.

[7] Ibid., p. 12.

[8] Ibid., p. 17.

[9] As a concrete proposal, the Note suggested that a Bokaro Project Committee be set up to expedite all decisions relating to the execution of the project without its being subject to the delays of existing procedural practices. This suggestion resulted in the formation in January, 1964, of Bokaro Steel Ltd., entrusted with the task of setting up the Bokaro Steel Plant, and of developing ancillary facilities such as the township and sources of supply of raw materials.

[10] The *68th Report* quotes the following extract from a letter dated October 7, 1963, by Mr. S. I. Malyshev, a member of the HSL Technical Committee and the top Soviet steel expert at Bhilai, to the Chairman of the Technical Committee: 'On going through the project report though in not much of the detail, I feel that the design organization (Dasturco) which prepared these materials are having all the potentialities to work out the final working drawings and also to supervise the progress of construction of the steel plant which must be built incorporating the last word in development of steel technology... . (*68th Report*, p. 9.) Thus, while the Soviet steel expert expressed confidence in Dasturco's ability to design and supervise the construction of Bokaro, his approbation did not characterize the Dasturco Report as 'first rate', as stated by K. V. Subrahmanyam, member of the Cabinet Sub-Committee on Science, in an article entitled 'The Tragedy of Bokaro', *Economic Times*, February 4, 1970.

[11] As a contrast, the Note cited (p. 6) that Kaiser of U.S.A. continued doing business elsewhere in spite of their assignment on the Tata Iron and Steel Company's expansion being delayed by five years on account of designing and other defects. The Note's assertion that competition would ensure the efficient designing and construction by Dasturco was however overdone. In actual practice, with increasing desire to import-substitute in consulting services and with only two agencies in existence — Dasturco in the private and the Central Engineering and Design Bureau in the public sector — the consulting assignments on future steel plants could be expected to be parcelled out between these agencies on a mutually acceptable basis.

[12] The Note cited several instances of operational difficulties created by the designing and selection of equipment unsuited for Indian conditions. One instance in the area of civil construction that arose out of inadequate arrangements and weak supervision on the part of a British Civil Engineering Company was the almost disastrous collapse of the piling foundations in the rolling mills area at Durgapur, the responsibility for the rectification of which had to be undertaken and guaranteed at great cost by the British Government itself.

Another instance referred to the eventual acceptance, after initial rejection, on the grounds of suitability to local conditions, by the Atlas Steel of Canada of the specifications prepared by Dasturco for the Alloy Steel Project at Durgapur.

[13] 'The Planning Commission Note on Bokaro', p. 7.

[14] The largest scope for import substitution was indicated in the area of *manufacturing* structurals. Indeed, it was emphasized that not only the setting up but the fabricating of structurals would be done by the same contractor in order to ensure speed and economy. Companies such as Braithwaite Burn and Jessop and Bridge and Roof were cited as having successfully undertaken such work earlier. It was also indicated that Indian manufacturers could supply cranes of 40 ton capacity or less which would represent about 10 percent of the value of the total crane requirements. Attention was drawn to Dasturco's suggestion to urgently set up fabricating capacity, so that cranes of heavier specifications could be manufactured indigenously.

[15] In this context, instances were cited of the Hindustan Construction Company who undertook all the civil work at Bhilai, Braithwaite, Burn and Jessop who executed similar work for the Indian Iron & Steel Company, and J.C. Gammons, who did the civil engineering work for the mills at Rourkela.

[16] 'The Planning Commission Note on Bokaro', p. 14.

[17] While the schemes outlined in its Notes by the Planning Commission, which is essentially a recommending body, are not binding, the 'Note on Bokaro', with its detailed suggestions, was crucial in view of the fact that for nearly three years after its submission, the efforts directed toward implementing the project were in line with the scheme outlined in the Note. Thus, after the failure of the proposal for American aid, attempts were continued in March-April 1964 for securing aid-financed *equipment only* from various sources such as England, Germany, and Japan. By that time, Dasturco had already (in July 1963) submitted their Detailed Project Report and an agreement was reached with the firm in April 1964 for its extensive participation in implementing the project. For details, see pp. 78-79.

[18] The implications of financing equipment purchases through aid from an alternative source, in case American aid did not materialize, or of procuring these through free foreign exchange, were not mentioned in the Note.

[19] It seems that the consulting role envisaged for Dasturco in Bokaro was in no small measure due to the personal interest of Prime Minister Jawaharlal Nehru. Thus, his death in May 1964 is mentioned as the turning point at which the reversal of Dasturco's role in Bokaro started. See, for example, K.V. Subrahmanyam, 'The Tragedy of Bokaro', *op. cit.*

CHAPTER 4

American collaboration on Bokaro

In May 1962, Dasturco was commissioned to prepare the Detailed Project Report on Bokaro. Around the same time, the U.S. Agency for International Development (AID) asked the U.S. Steel Corporation to make a feasibility study of the project. Both reports were submitted in 1963 (Dasturco's in July).[1] The following features of both reports are relevant in analyzing the reasons for the breakdown of U.S. collaboration on Bokaro.

(1) Dasturco estimated the cost of the project (excluding off-site facilities), with a capacity of 1.5 million tonnes for Stage I, at $ 751.47 million (Rs. 3.577 million), including a foreign exchange component of $ 318.48 million (Rs. 1.516 million).[2] According to the U.S. Steel Report, the corresponding figures for a Stage I capacity of 1.4 million tons were $ 919.428 million and $ 512.588 million.[3] Thus, the relative share of the foreign exchange component was 42 percent in the Dasturco Report and 55 percent in the U.S. Steel Report.

(2) Both reports indicated that the project would start making profits only at Stage II. Dasturco set full production at 4 million tonnes, while U.S. Steel gave the figure of 2.5 million tons. [4]

(3) In the Dasturco Report, the rated capacity of 1.5 million tonnes at Stage I was expected to be reached by 1969, and the rated capacity of 4 million tonnes for Stage II by 1976.[5] The U.S. Steel Report specified that the rated steel production of 1.4 million tons was to be reached by 1971, whereas the completion of the Stage II capacity of 2.5 million tons was expected by 1967 and the Stage III capacity of 4 million tons by 1980.

(4) Finally, to isolate the management of Bokaro from HSL, the U.S. Steel Report proposed that the management be entrusted to an American team for a period of ten years (presumably for the entire decade of the 1970's), at the end of which the rated capacity of 4 million tons would be set rolling. The maximum number of American technicians required during this period would be 670.[6]

These contrasts served as the backdrop to an ensuing drama which provided full play to the energies of powerful individuals, the political activity and lobbying of the economic interests concerned (especially the U.S. steel manufacturers) and the ideological arguments of both the U.S. Congress and the U.S. press in defense of the private sector. For almost a year, until the request for U.S. aid was withdrawn by the Government of India towards the end of 1963, there was considerable suspense and much speculation about whether U.S. aid would come through for Bokaro.

In this drama, the liberal and pragmatic forces, supporting the U.S. financing of Bokaro, and led by Ambassador Galbraith and President Kennedy himself, were pitted against the steel and shipping interests of the U.S. economy and the ideological opposition to U.S. support of public enterprises. We now proceed to analyze these forces and the sequence of events leading to the ultimate denouement.

Galbraith, Kennedy, and Bokaro
The cause of American collaboration for Bokaro was

advanced and pursued with tenacity, but unwarranted optimism, by John Kenneth Galbraith, Ambassador to India from April 1961 to July 1963.[7] Reading his *Journal*, one gets the impression that the proposal for American participation in Bokaro was for him a personal challenge which had possibilities of fulfillment. His arguments were non-ideological.

> This project is very important. It is needed, useful and sym-bolic. Many of the things we are doing are rather anonymous. We provide copper and other non-ferrous metals which are needed and useful but not very dramatic. And our past help to private-sector plants, such as Tata's has evoked the comment, 'The Americans help the Tatas and Birlas who are already rich. By contrast, the Soviets or British build plants that belong to the people.' Now we are in the same league — provided that we can perform.[8]

Galbraith, however, was aware of the difficulties of hammering out a concrete proposal that would meet both the U.S. collaborators' expectations of overriding control of the management of the project with a minimum finan-cial stake, and the Indian desire for maximum participa-tion in terms of consulting, supervision of construction, and supplies of indigenous equipment and materials. The first test of his negotiating abilities directed at averaging out these extreme positions was the original proposal 'for getting U.S. Steel in on the Bokaro mill as a private enter-prise operation'. It was characterized by Galbraith as a 'real bargain' for U.S. Steel.

> Of the $ 500 million required (by way of foreign exchange), $ 100 million would be subscribed in common stock and the rest as a loan, possibly guaranteed, from the United States and India. One third of the $ 100 million of common stock would be held by each of U.S. Steel, private Indian capitalists and the Indian Government. Half of U.S. Steel's investment would be cash, the rest in technology and 'know-how'. This means they would get control of a $ 500 million firm for ten years — their control is to be guaranteed for that time — for an investment of $ 16.7 million. A real bargain.[9]

Galbraith also realized that securing Indian acceptance of a
proposal so far short of their expectations would be a
problem, but he sounded optimistic about managing the
Indian side.

> The question is whether we can have a clear authority to build
> the steel mill and manage it for a running-in period. First, I
> must persuade Washington to provide the money. Then I must
> persuade the Indians. I do not have it until they agree to the
> appropriate conditions. Duplicity is not easily avoided. In this
> case, I am a little assisted by the fact that the Indians are on
> the defensive about the defective operation of the existing
> publicly-owned mills.[10]

Meanwhile, in the United States itself, American participation in Bokaro was being advocated persuasively by no less
a person than President John F. Kennedy. As early as
1958, when India was seeking an emergency foreign-
exchange transfusion to revive the almost moribund
Second Five-Year Plan, Senator Kennedy had cosponsored
with Senator John Sherman Cooper a resolution that urged
recognition by the U.S. Congress of 'the importance of the
economic development of the Republic of India to its
people, to democratic values and institutions, and to peace
and stability in the world'.[11] By 1962, the intellectual and
emotional commitment of President Kennedy to Indian
economic development was fortified by the need to coun-
ter increasing Soviet participation in the Indian economy
– especially in steel and machine-building.[12] The shib-
boleth against aid to the Indian public sector was to be
replaced by an attitude of selective participation, at least
in the steel industry, at the time that the Bokaro proposal
for U.S. aid came up. At a Washington press conference in
mid-May 1963, President Kennedy stated not only that
America should help the Indians build the Bokaro steel
plant, but that it should be supported in the public sector.
Ambassador Galbraith was ecstatic: 'It was a marvelous
no-nonsense statement.... Now he has moved in and

settled matters. He made the statement in a press conference'.[13]

A remarkably ill-judged statement indeed from an
articulate commentator on the ideology and the techno-
structures of the United States! For U.S. support for
Bokaro was to wither away within eight months of the
Presidential declaration which Galbraith assumed had
'settled matters' in his favor.

The U.S. Steel Industry, the U.S. Congress, the U.S. Press, and Bokaro

Besides Galbraith and the President, there were the powerful American steel and shipping interests, the American
Congress and its various Committees and the American
press. Their position on Bokaro was adamant and reflected
a complex set of considerations.

The first and most dominant consideration was essentially ideological, namely, that the commitment of about
half a billion dollars to a single steel plant in the Indian
public sector was contrary to the American 'way of life'.
The tone and content of this line of reasoning was initiated
by the arguments and recommendations of the Committee
to Strengthen the Security of the Free World headed by
General Lucius Clay. It stated that:

> The observation of countless instances of politically operated,
> heavily subsidized, and carefully protected insufficient state
> enterprises in less-developed countries makes us gravely doubt
> the value of such undertakings in the economic lives of these
> nations.... While we realize that in aiding foreign countries we
> cannot insist upon the establishment of our own economic
> system, despite its remarkable success and progress, we should
> not extend aid which is inconsistent with our beliefs, demo-
> cratic tradition, and knowledge of economic organization and
> consequences.... The only way the Congress can express its
> disapproval of a development loan project is through a specific
> prohibition in the authorization act. The committee is of the
> opinion that the Congress should have a strong voice in the
> decision as to how the United States taxpayers' money is to be
> spent overseas. As it is now, the executive has the sole
> authority for this decision.[14]

This ideological position, asserting the superiority of the private sector over the public sector in the underdeveloped countries in general and the Indian steel industry in particular, was taken up extensively in the U.S. press. A typical example is the following extract from the *U.S. News and World Report*.[15] It is hostile, opinionated, and inaccurate in places:

'The first [Indian] Government mill to be completed was financed by the Russians.... American engineers describe the mill as extremely simple in design, but it does produce steel. Their description expresses the view that the mill is built by peasants for peasants.[16]

'Russians have kept control of this whole operation, with the Indian general manager no more than a figurehead.[17]

'The German experience, by comparison, had been a nightmare.... Trouble developed and a special commission of German technicians was appointed to find out what was wrong. The Commission found: Indian personnel with adequate training was extremely scarce.... Absenteeism had risen to 25 percent. Hindustan Steel Ltd. had 3,600 headquarters personnel, and a minor decision required from 24 to 36 months. About 30 percent of Indians trained in Germany were given jobs for which they were not trained.[18]

'British experience at India's third Government steel mill is only a little better.[19]

'Private steel companies have the trained personnel, experience and means to expand to meet India's steel needs. Government stands in their way. The question is whether American taxpayers now will build new steel facilities to take the place of those that could be financed privately.[20]

'Indian officials already are wheeling out the whipsaw argument. They say that if the Americans do not go ahead with the project, then the Russians will.'

A similar ideological preference for the private sector

was voiced by the Sub-Committee of the House Committee on Appropriations of the U.S. Congress.[21] Galbraith's argument before this Sub-Committee that, while
the private sector steel plants were efficiently managed,
there was absolutely no scope for raising private funds for
Bokaro inside or outside India, was dismissed.[22] In other
words, the fact that the case for steel plants in the Indian
public sector arises largely from economic considerations
was overlooked.

Another consideration was the threat posed by Bokaro
specifically to U.S. shipping and steel interests. While this
argument was played up in the various House and Senate
speeches, on close examination it turns out to be both
overstated and irrelevant while considering U.S. commitment of funds for the steel plant. The Project Report
prepared by the U.S. Steel Corporation for Bokaro clearly
indicated that the Indian requirements of steel, even after
the completion of Bokaro, would substantially outstrip
Indian production, thereby requiring steel imports in
India. Second, as was pointed out by Galbraith in his
testimony before the House Sub-Committee, given the
Indian determination to build the plant Bokaro would be
set up in any case.

The only relevant argument in this context was the
extent to which U.S. financing (and hence aid-tying) of
Bokaro would benefit U.S. steel and heavy engineering
industries. Here again there was some difference of opinion
among the witnesses before the House Sub-Committee.
While Galbraith emphasized that the U.S. financing of
Bokaro would activate the capacities of the machine building industries in Western Pennsylvania, Ohio, Northern
Indiana, Illinois, and elsewhere,[23] and Mr. Clows, the
representative of the United Steelworkers of America, also
testified that U.S. aid-financed construction of Bokaro
would generate significant demands for U.S. steel, the
members of the House Sub-Committee chose to agree with
Mr. Obbard, the Executive Vice-president of the U.S. Steel

Corporation, who testified that the demand generated for U.S. steel by U.S. aid-financing of Bokaro would be marginal.

A final 'anti-collaboration' argument proceeded from the opposition that American credits to Bokaro would be an unsound investment. Members of the House Sub-Committee asserted that Bokaro was a pig in a poke. They seized on a statement in the U.S. Steel Corporation Project Report on Bokaro specifying that there were some problems relating to raw materials, transportation, skilled labor, and management which could bear further investigation.[24] Countering their argument, Mr. Gaud, the representative of the U.S. Agency for International Development, stated in his testimony: 'United States Steel looks at the proposition from the standpoint of an individual entrepreneur paying taxes and selling steel at the Government-controlled price. If, however, you look at the mill from the standpoint of the Government and the economy, where the selling price of steel exceeds the price paid to the producing mills, you will find that the mill will earn 22 percent before taxes, and 11 percent after taxes'.[25] In other words, Bokaro would be a viable project, if the rate of return were computed on the basis of the actual price of steel paid by the Indian consumers. Neither this argument, suggesting a more meaningful criterion for assessing Bokaro's profitability, nor Galbraith's pleas that the return to the American taxpayer should include the non-economic benefits of aiding a steel plant in the Indian public sector, thereby securing Indian goodwill and countering the Soviet aid-offensive, made any impact on the members of the House Sub-Committee.

Eventually, as a result of the Clay Committee recommendation arguing for Congressional control of aid disbursements, an amendment was introduced to the foreign aid bill in August 1963 by Senator William S. Broomfield. It sought specific approval from Congress for any single foreign aid commitment exceeding 100 million dollars.

This amendment was passed by the Congress.[26] A few weeks later, toward the end of 1963, the Government of India withdrew its request for American aid for Bokaro. This decision amounted to a recognition of the insurmountable difficulty in securing U.S. aid for Bokaro; and it was clearly dictated by the desire to avoid the certain alternative outcome of an *explicit* rejection by the U.S. which would have jeopardized the U.S. image in India yet more seriously.

Thus, the proposal for American aid for Bokaro, put forth with considerable optimism by India and sponsored in a spirit of commitment and pragmatism by Galbraith and Kennedy, was rejected at the American end essentially out of ideological considerations. It did not even come up for negotiations between the two governments. Even if it had, the course of the negotiations would have been far from smooth.

In the first place, an agreement on how Bokaro should be managed during and after its construction would have been difficult to reach. Having chosen to cooperate with the public sector in India, and thus made an ideological concession, the U.S. negotiators would certainly have sought maximum control over the management of Bokaro. An indication to this effect was given by Mr. Gaud in his testimony before the House Sub-Committee: 'We would not be prepared to go forward with this proposition until we had worked out a satisfactory understanding with the Indian Government as to U.S. personnel controlling the design of the mill, construction of the mill and a management contract for a period of five to ten years'.[27] True, both the Indian Planning Commission (in its Note on Bokaro) and the U.S. Steel Corporation Project Report stipulated that the project be managed by an independent organization. However, while the former was motivated by considerations of avoiding procedural delays, the latter insisted on complete control over the management of the project for ten years so as to put it onto a stable and efficient routine at the end of the period.[28] This strict turn-key concept of the U.S. Steel Corporation Report was completely at variance with that contained in the Planning Commission Note. The latter was rooted in the decision that Bokaro must blaze a trail different from that of the earlier steel plants: Bokaro had to be not merely designed and engineered by local enterprise but also managed, from the very beginning, by an Indian organization.

It is therefore highly unlikely that Dasturco would have been retained as consultant, designer, and construction supervisor for Bokaro if U.S. aid had come through. Take, for instance, the following definitive view expressed by Mr. Obbard, Executive Vice-President of the U.S. Steel Corporation, in his testimony before the House Sub-Committee:

> There is in India a reasonably good force of consulting and design engineers, but we think that while they would be entirely competent to carry out detailed design work, for a large and most modern mill of this sort which would employ U.S. equipment, U.S. engineering should be used... . The construction should be handled by large, competent outside concerns which can provide the supervision, the equipment, and the coordination that is so necessary to progress any large job satisfactorily.[29]

The overriding consideration of delivering Bokaro as a prestigious triumph of U.S. steel technology and management would certainly have gone against the U.S. preference for encouraging private initiative (in this instance, Dasturco).

An agreement on the possibility of maximizing the usage of Indian equipment and technicians would have been equally difficult to reach in view of the wide disparities between the U.S. Steel Corporation Report and comparable Indian estimates. The determination in the Planning Commission Note that Bokaro was to be an Indian-designed and Indian-built steel plant, extended also to the use of domestic equipment (especially of structurals), although the Note contained no concrete details on procuring equipment from local sources. The possibilities of disagreement on this aspect are reflected in the discrepancies of the estimated requirements of foreign exchange in the Dasturco and the U.S. Steel Corporation Project Report on Bokaro for the Stage I capacities of 1.5 million tons for the former, and 1.4 million tons for the latter. The relative share of the foreign exchange component was 42 percent in the Dasturco Report and 55 percent in the U.S. Steel Corporation Report. As Mr. Gaud stated in his testimony before the House Sub-Committee: 'The United States Steel people assumed that the entire mill, that all the equipment of the mill, would be made in the United States and that is how they got to their figure of $ 512 million foreign exchange.'[30] It is highly unlikely that the U.S. would have made significant concessions towards import substitution in equipment usage, considering that the Indian capacities for heavy machine building are Soviet-aided.

Next, consider the question of Indian steel technicians for Bokaro. While the Planning Commission Note placed these requirements at '30 to 40 top ranking foreign steel plant technicians to man the key posts at the Bokaro Project for a limited period of time', the U.S. Steel Corporation Report's estimated requirements during the ten year period was 670 at the maximum.

Finally, the technology recommended for Bokaro in the U.S. Steel Corporation Report was of the semi-continuous casting variety instead of the more advanced and efficient method of continuous casting of flat steel items.

In view of these indications, it is extremely unlikely that the critical features of the initial Indian conception of Bokaro could have been retained if an agreement had been reached for U.S. collaboration on the project.[31]

Notes to Chapter 4

[1] *68th Report*, p. 4.
[2] Ibid., p. 2.
[3] Ibid., p. 4.
[4] Ibid., pp. 3, 5.
[5] Ibid., pp. 2-3.
[6] Ibid., p. 6.

[7] Galbraith describes his efforts in his inimitable style: 'By a combination of persuasion, threats, blackmail, promises to resort to higher authority, appeals to patriotism and promises of what the Soviets will do, I seem to have a provisional approval of our financing of the fourth steel mill at Bokaro. Now we must find a way of building it with competence and distinction.' Cf. *Ambassador's Journal — A Personal Account of the Kennedy Years*, (London: Hamish Hamilton, 1969), p. 215.

[8] Ibid.

[9] Ibid., p. 240. This proposal, with a foreign exchange cost of $ 500 million and control over management of the project for ten years is contained in the Project Report submitted by the U.S. Steel Corporation.

[10] Ibid., pp. 216-217.

[11] Ved Mehta, 'A Reporter at Large, Indian Journal, Development: The Pulsating Giant', *The New Yorker*, February 14, 1970, p. 84.

[12] 'By 1962, India had received about four billion dollars from the United States, compared to only about eight hundred million dollars from the Soviet Union, but Soviet aid, with its dramatic industrial projects, was continuing to make the greater impression.' Ibid., p. 84.

[13] Galbraith, *Journal*, p. 572.

[14] The Committee submitted its report to President Kennedy in March 1963. It was appointed to study American military and economic assistance programs, reportedly 'in a vain attempt to placate the conservatives'. See P.J. Eldridge, *The Politics of Foreign Aid in India*, London School of Economics and Political Science (Vikas Publications, 1969), p. 32; the author also summarizes the Report thus: 'After a lightning world tour, the Committee produced a report which consisted of a series of dogmatic assertions based on unexamined assumptions.' Ibid., p. 32.

Galbraith found General Clay exasperating. Thus, he records: 'General Clay is heading a Committee to review the AID program. He has decided that there must be no assistance to Bokaro as long as it is in the public sector. In other words, for blatant ideological reasons, he is going back to the policies of the Eisenhower Administration: these were a grievous failure. Nothing substantial was done to advance private investment; and they talked about it enough to cause everyone to suppose our concern was to sustain capitalism rather than help the Indians. I have shifted to a purely pragmatic policy of doing whatever works. This even relaxes the tension on private enterprise.' Galbraith, *Journal*, p. 544. Galbraith characteristically overestimated his own strength and underrated the power of U.S. ideological and economic interests in thinking: 'I have written a careful rebuttal to Clay making it clear that he would lose sadly in any effort to carry his case to the public... . He has just joined Lehman Brothers in New York and will not want to start his banking career there with a public brawl. As for me I would welcome it.' Ibid., p. 544.

[15] *U.S. News and World Report*, April 15, 1963.

[16] A similar judgment on Bhilai was ascribed to German engineers: 'West German engineers say the Bhilai plant was developed by Krupp during the 1920's for the Russians. Since the Soviet Union was then, after the revolution, a developing country, the mill was left as simple as possible... . What the Soviets apparently had done, the Germans say, was to copy the original steel mill — adding some modifications — and duplicate it at Bhilai'. See Ernest Weatherall, 'German Backed Steel Mill Sets the Example of Hope in India'. *Christian Science Monitor*, April 16, 1969.

Both these judgments, slanderous in tone, overlook the fact that in the initial stages of mastering the steel technology, it may be a positive advantage to have a plant such as Bhilai with a simple technology, especially when the technology is suited for rolling out structural items of the kind manufactured by Bhilai. Further, it is naive to equate the 'latest' in technology with the 'most economical' — a fallacy which prevails among engineers and journalists and which, in this instance, was clearly fed by anti-Soviet and anti-Indian-Socialism sentiments.

[17] On the Indian scene, the Soviets have the best record in training Indian personnel and of systematically transferring responsibility to them.

[18] The problems with the German-aided Rourkela steel plant arise for the most part from its having been assembled by 300 German contractors without any one of them having the responsibility for its efficient functioning.

[19] The operation of the British-aided Durgapur steel plant, situated in the politically turbulent state of West Bengal, is plagued by perennial labor problems arising from rivalry between trade unions.

[20] While the two private steel plants in India have a long tradition

of efficient management, there is no evidence that they have either the trained manpower or the resources to undertake the required expansion of steel capacities in India. There is also no evidence that a concrete proposal for a new steel plant from the private sector was rejected by the Government of India. On the other hand, the Government did allow the Tata Iron and Steel Company to expand its capacities. In actual practice, the steel industry in India (comprising three plants in the public and two in the private sector) is consciously managed along oligopolistic lines with decisions on issues such as pricing, distribution, rolling programs, etc., made on the basis of joint consultations and consensus. Furthermore, the Indian private sector seems to regard the expansion of the steel industry in the public sector with approval, placing it in the same catagory as the expansion of electricity, transport, and other infra-structure items.

[21] Hearings before a Sub-Committee of the Committee on Appropriations, House of Representatives (hereafter referred to as the House Sub-Committee), Eighty-Eighth Congress, First Session, (Foreign Operations Appropriations for 1964), pp. 1520-1703. These are hereafter referred to as the House Sub-Committee Hearings.

[22] Ibid., p. 1544. Galbraith further emphasized that both J.R.D. Tata and Bharat Ram, two Indian industrialists, were strongly in favor of Bokaro being in the Indian public sector.

[23] For details, see his article, 'The Bokaro Steel Mill', *Washington Post*, August 1963, reproduced in the House Sub-Committee Hearings, pp. 1545-1547.

[24] The U.S. Steel Corporation Report refused to accept the Indian Steel Ministry's argument that these problems had been adequately investigated and that steps were already initiated for handling some of the inadequacies.

[25] Hearings of the House Sub-Committee, p. 1479.

[26] For a detailed and colorful documentation of these debates, see Ved Mehta, 'A Reporter at Large', *op. cit.*

[27] Hearings of the House Sub-Committee, p. 1397.

[28] Handing over the management of a four million ton steel plant to the U.S. collaborators for a period of ten years would also have implied certain undesirable possibilities from the Indian point of view, with respect to the pricing and distribution of flat steel products to be manufactured at Bokaro. Until recently, when controls on the distribution of all varieties of steel were reimposed because of general shortage, the trend (beginning with the recommendations of the Raj Committee Report on Steel Decontrol in 1964) was toward the gradual relaxation of controls in the distribution of all varieties

of steel except flat products where the shortages have been persistent. It is quite possible that with complete control on the management of Bokaro, specializing in flat products, the U.S. collaborators would have insisted on the relaxation of the remaining controls in the distribution of flat products. Such 'liberalization' measures — even when justified on economic grounds — are resented when the initiative for their implementation comes from a foreign source (as was illustrated by the controversy surrounding the devaluation of the rupee in June 1966).

[29] Hearings of the House Sub-Committee, pp. 1623-1624. Mr. Obbard's views are strikingly similar to those of Mr. Gubert, Director of the Soviet agency Gipromez, quoted on p. 44.

[30] Ibid., p. 1485.

[31] The *68th Report* devotes two pages out of a total of 114 to the entire episode of the proposal for U.S. collaboration on Bokaro. These two pages merely summarize some of the details of the U.S. Steel Corporation Project Report. There is no recounting of the series of events, including the debates in the U.S. Congress and its various committees, nor a statement of the reasons for which U.S. aid for Bokaro failed to materialize. This is a serious omission in a Report prepared by a Committee of the Lok Sabha. It is normally supposed to give an objective assessment of the subject under discussion. This omission cannot, however, be explained in terms of the composition of the Committee. Of the 15 members of the Committee, one each belonged to the Swatantra, D.M.K., S.S.P., and C.P.I. (M) parties, two each to the Jan Sangh and Congress (Organization) parties, and seven to the Congress (ruling) party. In the absence of any explicit political bias in the composition of the Committee, its pro-Dastur and hence anti-Soviet tone is to be explained in terms of a 'self-reliance for India' stand.

CHAPTER 5

Soviet collaboration on Bokaro

Early in March 1964, open tenders for the separate sections of the plant were invited from England, West Germany, Japan, and the Soviet Union. In April 1964, a draft agreement for engineering and consulting services for setting up the plant was initiated with Dasturco.[1] Dasturco was appointed consulting engineers for the 1.5 million tonne stage for a six-year period, starting from April 1964.

The Soviet offer of equipment for Bokaro in March was reportedly conveyed to the Indian Steel Minister by the Soviet Ambassador in person. The sequence of negotiations that followed resulted in full-fledged Soviet participation in the Bokaro steel plant. The process of negotiation brings out the constraints imposed on the Indian bargaining strength by several crucial policy objectives;[2] at the same time, Dasturco's cost reduction proposals[3] illustrate the limitations imposed on foreign collaborators in developing countries by the availability of local consulting firms, competent to judge the inadequacies of the proposed schemes for collaboration.

Chronology of Events Relating to Soviet Collaboration in Bokaro

Appendix I lists the series of events between the Soviet-Indian discussions in July 1964 and the signing of the second contract with Dasturco on February 25, 1967, after the agreement on Soviet collaboration had been finalized. It illustrates the main features of the negotiation process which indicate the constraints, at each stage, on Indian bargaining strength.

The Soviets made their offer of equipment in March 1964. The first official Indian delegation to Moscow in July 1964 argued that Dasturco be given 'large chunk' of consulting services (see Appendix I). When the Soviet team visited Delhi in August for technical discussions Dasturco, despite its six-year contract with the Indian Steel Ministry, was kept out of the discussions, presumably at Soviet insistence.[4]

The crucial event was the signing of the inter-governmental agreement for Soviet financial and technical aid in January 1965. The Soviet government extended up to 200 million rubles credit for meeting the foreign exchange costs of the steel mill. The credit was to finance purchases of Soviet equipment, as well as the required services. In effect, Dasturco's Detailed Projected Report was to be replaced by the Soviet agency Tiazpromexport's report, submitted on December 22, 1965.

In accepting the Soviet Project Report, the Indian government acted with uncharacteristic haste marked by procedural lapses. The twenty-eight volumes of the Soviet Report were 'looked over' by a government Technical Committee in five weeks. The inevitable impression is that this scrutiny was merely ritual. After accepting the Soviet Report on March 29, 1966, the Indian Steel Ministry asked Dasturco to submit cost reduction proposals *within seven weeks*. This emergency operation was required by a clause in the Memorandum of Acceptance of the Soviet Project Report which provided that the Soviet consultants would consider concrete technical suggestions for cost reduction which might be made by the Indian side *within three months.* An effort was clearly being made to minimize any genuine possibility of altering the Soviet Project Report. Finally, while Dasturco's Cost Reduction Study was still under preparation, agreements were signed with Soviet agencies for the supply of equipment, materials, working drawings, and services of Soviet specialists for the construction of the plant. The speed with which these crucial details were settled appears abnormal for India, where slowness of decision making and delays are not uncommon. That the Soviet negotiators applied energy, if not pressure, seems obvious.

Policy Objectives and Soviet Collaboration

The strategic policy objectives of the Indian steel industry placed certain constraints on the evolution and outcome of the Soviet-Indian negotiations on Bokaro and greatly affected the strength of the Indian bargaining position.

The consideration paramount to the growth of the Indian steel industry is that it should take place in the public sector. While this was one of the reasons for the failure of U.S. collaboration, it was certainly in keeping with Soviet attitudes toward participation in Bokaro. Indeed, the consolidation of the public sector agency, Central Engineering and Design Bureau (CEBD), and the establishment of Hindustan Steel Construction, Ltd. (HSCL), a public sector construction company,[5] probably resulted from Soviet cooperation. Furthermore, early in 1970, the Indian government concluded an agreement with the Soviet Union for the establishment of a refractories plant in the public sector.[6] Finally, an inter-governmental agreement of February 1970 stipulated that the Bokaro plant was to be constructed with a four, rather than the original 1.7, million tonne capacity. The CEDB, not Dasturco, was assigned to design this stage. These developments with Soviet cooperation unmistakably indicate that

the emphasis in the future growth of the Indian steel industry would be not only on India making steel but on the
Indian *public sector* making steel *from start to finish.*
While the proximate and apparent reason for setting up
and consolidating these services in the public sector was to
expedite the construction of Bokaro, the ultimate con-
sequence was the existence of public sector facilities to be
available for future expansion of the Indian steel industry.

It does not appear that Dasturco's ouster resulted from
the Indian negotiators' commitment to a possible objective
of 'steel in the public sector from start to finish'. From the
sequence of events, it is clear that the facilities for steel
building in the public sector were consolidated *after*
Dasturco was effectively removed from its original role in
Bokaro. However, three crucial factors are worth emphasizing.

First, while the Soviet Union does trade with private
business and extend technical know-how to private industry in developing countries, it explicitly prefers to con-
solidate the 'technostructure' in basic industries in the
public sector.

Second, although Dasturco was ousted early in the
process of negotiation, both sides had to contend with the
resulting controversy that continued in the Indian press
and Parliament. Consequently, while Tiazpromexport took
over Dasturco's design responsibilities for the first stage of
1.7 million tonnes, it became increasingly difficult to use
Soviet agencies for Dasturco's other services. Thus, as the
negotiations progressed, the HSCL was assigned the civil
construction work and the CEDB, the designing of
Bokaro's expansion. By legitimately starting the whole
controversy and then keeping it alive, Dasturco may have
unwittingly contributed to Bokaro's 'Indianization' and to
its implementation by public sector agencies.

Third, the Indian negotiators were undoubtedly motivated by the desire to solve a persistent problem plaguing
the Indian public sector, namely how to utilize the redun-

dant capacities and services in the Indian public sector. In the case of Bokaro, the problem was one of utilizing the services of the engineers, steel technologists and construction personnel which already existed and which were on the Government's payroll when the negotiations began.[7]

The second policy objective is the relentless pursuit of import substitution. The plants producing outputs which could be utilized for Bokaro such as the Heavy Electrical Equipment Plant (HEEP) at Hardwar, the HEC at Ranchi, the Mining and Allied Machinery Corporation (MAMC) at Durgapur, and the Kotah Instrumentation Plant are all Soviet-collaborated. Given the Soviet commitment to these plants in terms of both finance and prestige, the likelihood of their outputs being utilized to the maximum extent for Bokaro was highest under Soviet collaboration for Bokaro.

This is indicated to some extent by the differences in the relative magnitudes of the foreign exchange component in the total investment cost of the various project reports. While in Dasturco's Project Report the foreign exchange component for the first stage of 1.5 million tonnes was 42 percent of the total investment cost, the corresponding figures were 55 percent in the U.S. Steel Report for the first stage of 1.4 million tons and 21 percent in the Soviet Detailed Project Report for the 4 million tonne stage.[8] More concretely, while the Dasturco Project Report put the domestic content of equipment usage for the plant at 25 to 30 percent, it has been placed at 63 percent in the Soviet Project Report.[9]

Indeed, a crucial consideration underlying the decision (made in February 1970) to construct Bokaro with a continuous capacity of four million tonnes was the pressing need to activate the capacities of the HEC, HEEP, MAMC and the Kotah Instrumentation plant — especially after the recession of 1966.[10] The Soviet stake in and the Indian anxiety to utilize these capacities must have had a paramount influence on the course of the negotiations.

It should, however, be emphasized that there were two

alternative possibilities under Soviet collaboration which could have permitted the maximum possible usage of Indian fabricating capacities for Bokaro. These were (1) Dasturco making the required alterations in its Detailed Project Report to suit Soviet and especially HEC specifications; or (2) the Soviet consultants themselves making marginal alterations in the Dasturco Detailed Project Report. While both these proposals were considered, they appear to have been shot down by the Soviet negotiators with the argument that the suppliers of equipment are required under contract to give performance guarantees and that these guarantees can be given only if the Project Report is prepared in detail according to Soviet norms, standards, and specifications. More specifically, the Director of Gipromez, Mr. Gubert, is reported to have insisted on the inevitability of linking the supplies and the designing of equipment, not because Dasturco were not good enough but because 'the project report of Dasturco has been prepared on the basis of equipment not being manufactured in the USSR. Such a big work like Bokaro should be done only by big agencies in close and continuous collaboration with the equipment manufacturers'.

In effect, the Soviet negotiators succeeded in making their activization of Soviet-aided steel making capacities in India conditional on their being allowed to do the Detailed Project Report for Bokaro. What was overlooked by the Indian side was the fact that the Soviet Union, with its commitments both of finance and prestige in these capacities, would have wanted to activate them in any case. In other words, the objective of import substitution could have been a binding constraint on the course of the negotiations only when settling the details of a *non-Soviet* aid-offer for Bokaro.[11] Therefore, in insisting on acquiring the consulting and designing jobs for Bokaro, and tying it with the activization of heavy engineering capacities in India, the Soviet negotiators were not making an offer of the 'take it or leave it' variety.

However, the Indian side was not in a position to insist: 'We will not take it because. . . '. The fact of the matter is that while managing these negotiations, the Indian delegations were equipped neither with a concrete proposal from an alternative foreign source for supplies of foreign equipment nor with the counter-argument that the purchases of foreign equipment would be financed from a non-Soviet source with free foreign exchange or with suppliers' credit.

Indeed, the final policy consideration relevant to the course of the negotiations is that while steel in the public sector has been assigned a high priority in Indian planning, the foreign exchange needs of the three steel plants have been met with foreign aid and not through the use of free foreign exchange.

An exception to this pattern was not considered for Bokaro, presumably for three reasons: (1) In the first place, having secured foreign aid for the Bhilai, Durgapur, and Rourkela steel plants from three different sources, the Indians were confident that foreign funds would come through for Bokaro as well. When the Soviet offer of equipment for Bokaro was made in April 1964, it was thought best to negotiate it rather than consider spending free foreign exchange for the project's import needs. (2) With plans of building substantial steel capacities in the future, it was thought that spending foreign exchange on Bokaro would have set up an undesirable precedent. (3) Finally, there was some oppositon to Bokaro arising from regional demands arguing against the locking up of resources in a massive project.[12] Given this phenomenon, any proposal to finance its import needs through free foreign exchange would have made Bokaro's acceptance even more difficult.

These arguments could have been countered. The first could have been disposed of in terms of a decision to reject any aid that was conditional on dispensing with the services of Dasturco. Regarding the second argument, with Bokaro providing the compulsions for the activation and

confident utilization of steel-building capacities in India,
the import needs for future steel plants could be minimized by invoking the indigenous availability rule with
greater assertion than is currently applied in permitting
steel plant equipment imports. As for the final argument,
the fact that Bokaro was already accepted as a project for
inclusion in the Fourth Five-Year Plan (originally beginning in April 1966) gave sufficient maneuverability in
financing its foreign exchange needs.

Besides, the financing of the foreign exchanges requirements of Bokaro spread over a period of, say, five years
through a provision of free foreign exchange appeared
manageable. These requirements ranged from approximately 200 million dollars in the Indo-Soviet agreement to
318 million dollars in the Dasturco Project Report and 512
million dollars in the U.S. Steel Corporation Project Report. If Dasturco's figure is adopted as the relevant one
and spread over a period of five to seven years, it would
work out to about 45 to 64 million dollars a year. This is
three to four percent of the average annual export earnings
of 1.5 billion dollars during 1960-66. This would appear to
be a manageable figure, especially if its spending was argued in terms of utilizing indigenous technical know-how
in line with the Planning Commission Note on Bokaro, and
more fundamentally, in terms of utilizing Dasturco, for
whose extensive services a six year contract was already
signed.

Even the more feasible alternative of meeting the import
needs of the plant through suppliers' credit was not considered. In other words, at no stage was the Soviet insistence on doing Bokaro as a turnkey job countered with
concrete alternatives. Throughout the negotiations, the
Soviet Union was treated as a lender of the last resort;
there was, therefore, heavy reliance on Soviet goodwill.

Notes to Chapter 5

[1] For details of this agreement, see pp. 78-79.

[2] A detailed analysis of these objectives follows in the concluding part of this chapter.

[3] For details, see Chapter 6.

[4] Even if Dastur had been physically present throughout the course of the Indian-Soviet negotiations, the final outcome, which led to the virtual displacement of Dasturco as consultants for and designers of Bokaro, would probably have been the same. (1) In the discussions in which he did participate, the Soviet technical team rejected most of his firm's cost reduction proposals. (2) Also, the role of Indian failure to present a unified, articulate case before the Soviet negotiators should not be exaggerated. To try to explain Dasturco's displacement in terms of the feud between Dastur and Mr. Wanchoo, the Secretary of the Steel Ministry (so vividly described in the *68th Report* and presented in Appendix I), would be simplistic and misleading. While these feuds provoked the Lok Sabha Committee to lay down the obvious and now generally accepted rule that technocrats, not bureaucrats, should lead technical discussion, and while they certainly affected the style of the negotiations, they could not have significantly affected their course and content. Concentration on these factors detracts attention from the inherent limitations on the strength of the Indian bargaining position, which are analyzed at length later on in this Chapter.

[5] For a detailed description of the CEDB and the HSCL, see Appendix II.

[6] The decision to set up refractories capacity in the public sector was apparently motivated by the failure of private suppliers to carry out the schedule of supplies for the construction of Bokaro. (For details of the backlog and reasons for it, see pp. 74-75.) As a remedy for this failure, the Secretary of the Steel Ministry stated before the Committee on Public Undertakings that the setting up of refractory capacity in the public sector would be actively considered (*68th Report*, p. 54). The Committee, however, expressed the opinion that in view of the already adequate private sector capacity to meet the steel industry's requirements, based on the current pattern of demand for various types, the decision to set up a refractories plant in the public sector should be taken only after a suitable inquiry into the problems of the private refractory suppliers. (Ibid., p. 55.)

[7] Given the explicit declaration of setting up an additional steel capacity of one million tonnes per annum in the decade of the seventies, the simultaneous existence of steelmaking expertise in the public and private sectors raises certain interesting possibilities. In

the first place, the designing and engineering of new steel plants would have to be parceled out between the CEDB and Dasturco. The indications are that in the immediate future, with the CEDB engaged fully in the designing of Bokaro's expansion, there would be adequate work for Dasturco in designing part of the new capacity. Of the three steel plants recently announced, to be located respectively at Salem in Tamil Nadu, Hospet in Mysore, and Visakhapatnam in Andhra Pradesh, it was reported that Dasturco will be consultants for two steel plants including the one at Salem, whereas the CEDB will handle the consulting of the third plant (see the *Times of India* (Delhi), June 5, 1970). However, in the long-run 'steady state' expansion of the steel industry in India, the possibility of active competition between the two consulting agencies may be deliberately discouraged by the determined policies aimed at keeping public sector capacities utilized.

On the other hand, with increasing political decentralization and with sanctioned steel plants affording opportunities to State governments for political assertions, the State governments may prefer to have 'their' steel plants designed by a private sector agency such as Dasturco rather than by a Central government designing agency such as the CEDB. The implications of the existence of multiple elements with possibilities of confrontation between the private sector and the public sector, and between the State governments and the Central government, are analyzed with reference to the working of the HEC at Ranchi by Dilip Mukherjee in 'Ranchi: A Fine Plant in the Wrong Setting', *Statesman* (Delhi), January 19, 1967.

It would be interesting to speculate if within the CEDB, the availability of steel technologies from as many as four sources would promote the adoption by future Indian steel plants of optimum technology. There are at least three reasons why this may not happen. First, a restrictive clause in the collaboration agreement itself would prevent the fabrication of their rolling mill designs by the HEC, which is Soviet-collaborated. For example, the agreement with the United Engineering and Foundry Company of America prohibits the fabrication of their rolling mill designs by the HEC, which is Soviet-collaborated. Second, the decision about which technology to adopt may be taken not by the specialists in the CEDB but by the bureaucrats in the HSL, which is in overall charge of the steel plants. It was reported that with the intention of promoting efficient choice of technology, a proposal to make the CEDB independent of the control of HSL is being seriously considered (see the *Times of India* (Delhi), April 17, 1970). Third, an interlocking of the source both for the design and its fabrication may encourage the adoption of a second-best technology. For example, a Gipromez design may be adopted because of the certain possibility of its fabrication at HEC.

[8] The investment cost of the project in the Soviet Detailed Project Report for the four million tonne stage was put at Rs. 7,700 million. The ruble credit announced for the plant was Rs. 1,666 million.

[9] The supplies of equipment and structurals from the various public sector units for the first stage of Bokaro have been placed at 41 and 73 percent respectively, out of the total estimated procurements from Indian sources of 63 and 91 percent respectively. The HEC and MAMC (both Soviet-aided) are expected to supply 82,906 tonnes of equipment out of the total of 90,329 tonnes, to be supplied by the public sector. (For more details, see the *68th Report*, pp. 43-44.)

[10] It seems that this was the overriding factor affecting the phasing of Bokaro capacities. Moreover, the announcement of the agreement with the provision associating the CEDB, an Indian public sector agency, with the designing of the extension was also aimed at placating nationalist sentiments. The impact of steel requirements on the scheduling of Bokaro capacities was secondary. This point was raised earlier in footnote 15, p. 12.

[11] The following paragraph in the *68th Report* clearly indicates that the course of the negotiations and especially the content of the inter-Governmental agreement for Soviet financial and technical aid were affected by considerations of utilizing domestic steel fabricating capacities: 'Inter-Governmental agreement signed between the Government of India and the Government of U.S.S.R. on 25th January, 1965, envisaged that the Indian and the Soviet sides will promote maximum participation of Indian Organizations in the designing of the works and the supply of equipment and materials because in both the fields it was stated that a large capacity existed in the country'. (See p. 13 of the *68th Report*.)

[12] These details were documented earlier on pp. 8-9.

CHAPTER 6

Dasturco's cost reduction study on Bokaro[1]

On May 29, 1966, the Government of India approved the
Soviet Project Report on Bokaro. On the same day, the
Steel Ministry wrote to Dasturco asking it to submit concrete proposals indicating possible cost reductions in the
Report. It was given seven weeks to accomplish this task,
which involved a scrutiny of the 28-volume Soviet Report.[2]

The Cost Reduction Study addressed itself to the following questions:

(1) What modifications could be made in the suggested
technologies? According to the Study, the two to three
percent rise per annum in steel plant equipment and construction costs in recent years was effectively neutralized
'by major advances in technology and by the adoption of
large unit equipment capacities both of which have tended
to lower capital cost per unit of installed capacity.'[3] Therefore, it was crucial to find out if the Soviet Project Report
recommended advanced technologies in the various units
of the Bokaro Steel Mill.

(2) Was the Soviet Project Report deficient with respect
to the suggested available supply and utilization of raw
materials such as coal, iron ore, etc.?

(3) The foreign exchange component of the steel plant in the Soviet Report was about 20 percent of the proposed investment cost of Rs. 7,700 million for the four million tonne capacity. Did the Soviet Report make maximum allowance for the utilization of indigenous equipment and raw materials, consulting and construction services, and technical expertise?

(4) Was it possible to lower costs by reducing or completely eliminating facilities and utilities not strictly required for the efficient operation of the plant?

(5) Was it possible to reduce costs by suggesting justifiable reductions in the costs/prices of equipment, materials, and services?

The Technologies proposed for Bokaro in the Soviet Project Report

Since rolling flat steel products is a complicated operation that involves a sequence of various operations in separate sections, each of which has a technology of its own, one must ask: how do the technologies proposed by the Soviet Report for the coke oven plants, the blast furnaces and sinter plants, the rolling mills, the water cooling system, etc., compare with the most advanced technologies available for *each* section? The Cost Reduction Study provides the answers with considerable objectivity and expertise.

It describes the Soviet Report's design for the blast furnace and sinter plant as excellent and comments on the proposed design of the coke oven plant:

> The coke oven and by-product plant proposed in the Soviet Report incorporates special features such as large size ovens, fast working machines, mechanised door cleaning arrangement and high speed crushers. The process control system is comprehensive and will ensure smooth operation of the plant. The by-product plant has been designed with a view to maximise the recovery of benzol and tar products. Elaborate laboratory and sampling facilities have been provided.[4]

However for the proposed steel melting shops and the rolling mills major technical modifications were recommended. For the four million tonne stage the Soviet Project Report provided for two separate steel melting shops. The first was to have five 100-tonne converters in the initial stage and the second, two 250-tonne converters in the next stage. The reason given for not installing the 250-tonne converters in the first stage itself was that the operation of such large converters was not yet fully established in the USSR.

The Study argued instead in favor of installing large-sized converters at the initial stage itself, stating that the advantages arising from economies of scale of large-sized converters were compelling:

> The reasons for adoption of 200 to 300 ton converters are that investment is lower (per annual ingot ton), operations are no more difficult than with smaller vessels, refractory consumption decreases, handling of hot metal, scrap, fluxes, slag and ingot moulds is simplified, and finally operating costs are lower.

The argument was further bolstered by evidence indicating a world trend toward larger sized converters:

> The world trend is, however, to adopt converters of 200 to 300 ton capacity for larger new plants of the type visualised at Bokaro and there are as many as 17 plants (13 in operation and 4 under installation) in the United States, Australia, Belgium, Germany and Italy with converters of this size; by the time Bokaro is commissioned there would be many more.[5]

The Study further emphasized the feasibility of acquiring larger-sized converters for Bokaro:

> In this connection it may be mentioned that the Austrian firm of Voest, originators of the LD process, has recently supplied a converter shop to the Soviet Union and they have also built large converters (333 metric tons, each) at Taranto, Italy. Voest has experience in India having built the Rourkela con-

verter shop and is now collaborating on the Triveni Structurals Project (a public sector company) which will fabricate heavy structurals and vessels. Government must take a view on whether by utilising the expertise of the Soviets and firms such as Voest/Triveni, converter size could not be enlarged to the overall benefit of Bokaro.[6]

The difference between the proposed Soviet design of two shops (with five 100-tonne and two 250-tonne converters), at a cost of Rs. 467.6 million, and Dasturco's design of one shop with four 250-tonne converters, at a cost of Rs. 289.6 million, was Rs. 187.2 million. The Study estimated the cost of acquiring all the necessary components for the alternative design through free foreign exchange at Rs. 50 million.[7]

In his evidence before the Committee on Public Undertakings (C.P.U.), Dr. Dastur stated:

> They [the Russians] have given us an antiquated design for the L.D. Plant. These 100 ton L.D. converters are not used for a big plant like this (Bokaro). Not that they are not used. If you want a plant of ¼ or ½ million tonnes, they can be used. But today 300 tonne L.D.s are absolutely standard and with one L.D. converter you get more than two million tonnes of steel. Here to get 1.7 million ingot tonnes they are putting up four or five 100 ton L.D. converters. It increases your capital cost and also your operating cost.[8]

The proposed modifications for the steel melting shops were not accepted by the Soviet side. In this connection, the *68th Report* of the C.P.U. reproduces the explanation given by the Soviet expert before the Technical Committee that scrutinized the Soviet Detailed Project Report:

> We can supply to India all the equipments which have been thoroughly checked up in operation in the Soviet Union. We can supply only equipments which can be commissioned straightaway and which can be easily mastered on the basis of our experience at our own steel plants. We are producing 100 ton converters. Today we are not in a position to supply India other converters of higher capacities. The 250 tonne con-

verters are now being installed in some of the steel melting shops and we will be in a position to supply them to India after we have gained enough experience in their operations. For the second stage we will be able to supply you such converters.[9]

An equally damaging criticism of the proposed slabbing mill was levelled by the Study. It was stated to be too large. Also, the recent applications of the method of continuous casting were likely to render the proposed Soviet mill technologically obsolete.[10]

Discussing the feasibility of getting a modified slabbing mill from the Soviet Union, the Cost Reduction Study stated that 'the technique has been well developed in the USSR and adopted at several plants... '.[11] More specifically, it indicated that at the Novo Lipetsk plant, an 'LD converter shop and wide strip mill are now under completion together with a continuous casting plant in preference to a slabbing mill'.[12]

The Soviet side rejected the alternative size of the slabbing mill proposed by Dasturco, insisting that their mill was not only just the right size for the job but also that the savings expected from the adoption of the alternative design would be marginal.[13] For the first stage of 1.7 million tonnes, the ultimate decision was to adopt (1) small converters in the steel-melting shops and (2) a massive slabbing mill, thereby rejecting the continuous casting method which eliminates the need for a slabbing mill altogether. Thus, the Soviet negotiators created the impression that the technologies relating to the adoption of large sized converters and the continuous casting method were of recent origin and that the Soviet Union had only just begun implementing these in its steel plants. Therefore, it seemed futile to insist that the Soviets should have done better than the best they could do by their own admissions.

In order to reach an objective judgment on these issues, it is crucial to analyze them from the following perspective: Having chosen to restrict the financing of the equipment requirements (and hence the technology) for Bokaro to aid-financed sources from the Soviet Union, was it possible for India to obtain advanced technologies from Soviet sources? In other words, were the Soviet team's arguments refuting the proposed alternatives of the Cost Reduction Study legitimate given the current state of technology in the Soviet steel industry? More specifically, would the Soviet planners consider adopting small sized converters and a massive slabbing mill for a steel plant of the size and type of Bokaro proposed to be installed in the Soviet Union itself?

The answer to this set of questions is provided by a Study entitled *Continuous Casting of Steel in the USSR — A Survey*, published by the OECD in 1964.[14] Regarding converter sizes, the evidence contained in this Study indicates that although the largest converters in operation in the Soviet Union in 1964 were of 55-ton capacity, 100- to 130-ton capacity vessels were likely to become standard units in the new converter bays with a typical capacity of 2.1-2.2 million tons. Moreover, the installation planned before 1964 for the Azovstal works was to consist of five converters, each of 250-ton capacity (to be increased to 300 tons). Again, the converter sizes already planned by 1964 for the new Novo Lipetsk plant's second stage of 3.8 million tons per annum was to have three converters of 250-ton capacity each.

According to the OECD Study, by 1960 the various economic and technical advantages of the continuous casting method were widely acknowledged by Soviet experts, and as of 1964, the declared Soviet plan was to increase the capacity of continuous casting installations in the Soviet steel industry from the 1963 level of two million tons to 22 million tons per annum in 1967. In this connection, the OECD Study states:

Full acceptance of the process at planning and decision-making
levels and determination to use it wherever possible could
hardly be more strongly demonstrated. Moreover, although
conditions in established industries outside the USSR are in
certain respects rather different, it is of note that this level of
acceptance of the process as a production method is far greater
than can be generally found elsewhere at present.[15]

Furthermore, the OECD Study cites detailed cost reductions worked out by Gipromez (the Soviet Design Institute
for Steel Plants) and cited by various Soviet sources, which
would result from the elimination of slabbing mills. More
concretely, the first stage of the new Novo Lipetsk plant,
already under construction in 1964 and expected to be
completed in 1965, was being built without any provision
for a slabbing mill.

It is therefore clear that if a plant like Bokaro were to
be set up in the Soviet Union, it would have been designed
in 1964 (and definitely in 1966 when the proposals of the
Cost Reduction Study were being discussed) with a provision for large-sized converters and without any provision
for a slabbing mill. The Soviet team's arguments that the
relevant technologies were in an experimental stage in the
Soviet Union created the rather misleading impression that
the Soviet Union did not want to 'learn by other people's
undoing' by trying out these technologies at Bokaro. On
the contrary, it is almost certain that in view of the
massive reliance placed on these new technologies for steel
output expansions in the Soviet Union, the Soviet negotiators were keen to avoid overburdening the Soviet capacities for turning out large-sized converters and continuous
casting equipment with additional demands for these for
setting up a steel plant in India. In this connection, it is
relevant that the OECD Study notes that while there were
six design and research institutes, eleven metallurgical
works (i.e., production plants), and a number of machine
construction works such as Uralmash, Yuzhuralmash,
Dnepropetrovskii works, and other engineering works in

the Soviet Union, there was a reported shortage of designers and research scientists in these organizations.

Availabilities and Utilization of Raw Materials Proposed
for Bokaro in the Soviet Project Report
The Cost Reduction Study made significant recommendations with respect to the sources and qualities of raw materials indicated in the Soviet Project Report. According to
the Study, it would be difficult to meet the coke requirements specified in the Report even if coke were made from
only the best quality coals in the country.[16] Because the
dual coal blends proposed by the Soviet Report threatened
to use up the best of the limited coking coals in India, the
Study proposed mixing a third blend of inferior variety
and adopting selective preparation techniques with a view
to improving coke strength. However, the feasibility of
acquiring the equipment for selective preparation of coke
from Soviet and Indian sources appeared rather limited.[17]

With respect to iron ore, the assessments of the Soviet
Report appeared to exceed the possible availabilities. The
Soviet Report envisaged larger deposits and richer ores
than those estimated by the Indian Bureau of Mines.[18]
Again, the performance rating of the blast furnace was
specified on the basis of extremely stringent variations in
ore content, although the Report stated that actual variations might turn out to be higher.[19] The Study insisted
that the blast furnace ratings and outputs be accurately
specified *in advance* in view of the certainty of high varia-
tion of ore content, especially in view of the fact that in
existing Indian steelworks, consistently good quality iron
has been difficult to produce.

Utilization of Equipment and Services from Domestic
Sources Proposed for Bokaro in the Soviet Project Report
We now consider if the Soviet Project Report allowed for
the maximum utilization of domestic availabilities. In this
connection, the recommendations of the Cost Reduction

Study ranged from the utilization of indigenous capacities in refractories and maintenance and spare parts to the fullest possible association of domestic consulting, engineering, and construction services with the project. Thus, it was suggested that the Project Report's provision for elaborate facilities in a central refractory shop be minimized, so that the bulk of the requirements could be purchased from the Indian refractory industry.[20] The Cost Reduction Study also proposed that the provision for a repair and maintenance shop with a cost estimate of Rs. 316 million be drastically reduced because the bulk of the equipment for Bokaro was proposed to be manufactured indigenously in public sector units which could also, therefore, supply spare parts and maintenance requirements.

However, the Study directed its most extensive and convincing arguments against the Soviet Project Report's excessive provision for importing consulting and specialists' services, especially during the construction of the project. Thus, the Soviet agencies were to be paid Rs. 36 million for the preparation of working drawings for the 1.7 million tonne stage, in addition to the Rs. 25 million they had already received for the preparation of the Detailed Project Report. The contract with the equipment suppliers provided for the 'technical' services of 450 to 500 Soviet specialists at the peak of construction activity, in addition to the services of 'suppliers' representatives' and other service personnel.[21] 'It is estimated that the expenses on account of the Soviet specialists, suppliers' representatives and service personnel and their families will be of the order of Rs. 123 million for the first stage, with about Rs. 15 million being incurred in Roubles.'[22] The Study proceeded to suggest that 'the bulk of the work for which such large amounts are to be paid (including foreign exchange) is essentially local work and could be competently undertaken by the Indian side which has greater familiarity with Indian conditions and practices and at a relatively lower cost'.[2 3] It accordingly proposed that 'the Soviet specialists for engineering and erection services be reduced to one-third the number, with [a] proportionate decrease in [the] requirements of service personnel, but with no change in the commissioning specialists'.[2 4]

At the basis of the massive divergences in the requirements for technical and managerial personnel, specified in the Soviet Project Report and Dasturco's estimates were, of course, two different conceptions of the steel plant. The Soviets clearly had in mind a turn-key type of assignment, whereas the Indian planners had conceived the plant as essentially Indian in execution. The crucial feature of a turn-key project is the extent to which its construction and management are handled by foreign technical and managerial personnel until the management is passed over ultimately to the local counterparts. While Bokaro, as eventually implemented, was to be a full-scale turn-key project, the turn-key elements in it in terms of the contribution of Soviet technical and supervisory personnel were definitely more substantial than envisaged in the Planning Commission Note. An important index of this was the reversal of Dasturco's role between the signing of the first consulting agreement with the firm on April 1964 and the second on February 25, 1967 *after* the collaboration agreement with the Soviet Union was signed.[2 5]

It must however be emphasized that excessive consulting, management, and designing fees by a ·donor country would have been a normal feature of any aid-financed agreement for Bokaro. Thus, while the expenses of Rs. 564.67 million for fees, design, engineering, supervision, and construction equipment were about 7 percent of the total plant cost of Rs. 7,700 million in the Soviet Project Report for the four million tonne stage, the provision of 109.4 million dollars for this item was as high as 15 percent of the total plant cost estimate of 746.3 million dollars by the U.S. Steel Corporation Report for the first stage of 1.4 million tons.

Facilities Proposed for Bokaro in the Soviet Project Report Which Were Treated as Redundant by the Cost Reduction Study

The Study made sweeping recommendations for reducing, and in some cases eliminating, several facilities. It was argued that, in some cases, these facilities incorporated a fantastic amount of built-in potential for capacity expansion with the result that they pushed up costs in the short as well as in the long run, because of the risk of technical obsolescence.[26]

The proposed strip mill was cited by the Study as one instance of the pursuit of massiveness. According to the Study, the Soviet Project Report did not give reasons for the selection of such a huge strip mill nor were the schedules of the rolling programmes indicated.

> ...the maximum capacity of the strip mill would only be realised in about 1980. It is to be considered whether there is any advantage in letting such a large investment remain only partially utilised for 15 years.[27]

Accordingly, the Study proposed that the size of the mill rolls and the capacity of the mill motors be reduced, and that the seventh stand in the strip finishing mill be eliminated, thereby leading to savings of Rs. 400 to 500 million. The Soviet technicians, while rejecting these proposals, contended that they had selected the size of the mill rolls in accordance with the latest trends. They also argued that if the size were reduced, the stiffness of the mill would be impaired, thus affecting the quality and yield of the strips. Moreover, they furnished detailed technical reasons for not accepting reductions in the capacity of the mill motors. They agreed only to the postponement of the seventh stand in the strip finishing mill to the second stage, with consequent savings of Rs. 10 million for the first stage.[28]

Some other facilities were considered redundant because they generated outputs which would be difficult to market or which could more profitably be produced elsewhere. In

the first category were the elaborate facilities for the
recovery of by-products such as ammonium sulphate,
benzol,[29] and tar products, all increasingly difficult to
market because of growing competition with similar products produced by the petro-chemical industries.

Again, the study suggested scrapping the fifth blast
furnace, which was intended primarily to produce foundry
iron for sale in the second stage of the project. This suggestion, based on an evaluation of projected demands for
foundry iron, was significant because the demand for
foundry iron is fairly widespread in India.[30] The proposed elimination of the fifth blast furnace in the second
stage would, correspondingly, eliminate one coke oven
battery and one sinter stand, leading to a cost reduction of
about Rs. 300 million.

All of the Study's estimates that related to this proposal
were challenged by the Soviet experts. They argued that
the omission of the fifth blast furnace would result not
only in reduced production of foundry iron but also in
reduced steel output by 150,000 to 200,000 tonnes at the
4 million tonne stage. It would also result in an adverse gas
balance, thus requiring a provision of approximately
100,000 tonnes of fuel oil, against the 75,000 tonnes
estimated by the Study. In any case, the proposal had no
bearing on the first stage, so it was not pressed by the
Indian delegation.

We might also note here the Study's proposal for the
adoption of a decentralized water supply and circulating
system with a cooling tower and a small balancing reservoir
instead of the Soviet Report's massive, centralized pond-
cooling system with only partial cooling in towers. The
Study indicated that the cost of the cooling tower system
would be 70 to 80 percent lower (as against the Soviet
Project Report estimate of 25 percent) than that of the
pond-cooling system. In rejecting the alternative system
proposed by the Study, the Soviet experts maintained that
(1) the Study had assumed better performance capabilities

for their own system than was actually possible; (2) the estimates of power consumption for the proposed alternative were unjustifiably low; (3) the savings in capital investment were overestimated; (4) while the Soviet design provided facilities for storing water for 30 days, the alternative proposal provided storage facilities for 20 days; and (5) the tower system proposed by the Study would require a larger servicing staff. While they agreed with the final argument, the Indian experts maintained that the overall operating costs of the tower system would be lower.[31]

The Study also cautioned against excessive staffing of Bokaro during its construction. It emphasized that in view of the difficulties of retrenchment, construction personnel are normally retained during the operating stage of Indian steel mills even though their productivity is doubtful.[32]. The need for some adjustment was stressed also on the ground that while the direct costs of labor per tonne of steel were small, substantial indirect costs arose from provisions for housing and welfare and, above all, from the cost-inflating task of having to manage a large labor force. The proposed adjustments in manpower requirements were also in tune with a highly mechanized and automated plant like Bokaro. Accordingly, the requirements were scaled down from 5,700 to 2,300 in the repair and maintenance complex. 'On the other hand the provision for top managerial staff has been increased from 600 in the Soviet report to 1,000 for this study.'[33]

The Cost Reduction Study completely eliminated the provision of Rs. 50 million made in the Soviet Project Report for safeguards against seismic forces at Bokaro. It was argued that the flexibility inherent in the single-storied, steel-framed buildings that predominated at the plant was adequate for meeting possible danger arising from this factor. They implied an outright cost reduction of Rs. 50 million.

Overpricing of Equipment and Services Proposed for Bokaro in the Soviet Project Report:
The Study made few recommendations on overpricing. It was handicapped by the fact that 'estimates in the Soviet report do not give cost details. Although the Soviet representatives were requested by Bokaro Steel to furnish capital cost breakdowns in the same detail as in the previous Dasturco Report, such information has not been available for the study. This has made the task of quantifying the cost savings difficult'.[34] On the other hand, that the Soviet Project Report did not link proposed expenditures to individual items provided the opportunity for a windfall suggestion that the provision of Rs. 458 million for 'minor construction work' (estimated at about 15 percent of major construction work) be deleted. 'The provision of a large amount under a miscellaneous head is not understood when construction quantities have been estimated in a detailed project report, and unforeseen expenses have also been separately provided at Rs. 385 million.'[35]

Finally, certain adjustments in the proposed estimates of construction work arose from the application of more realistic rates for basic civil engineering materials and labor in the Bokaro area.[36]

In summary, against a saving of Rs. 1,075 million worked out by the Cost Reduction Study, the net reduction agreed upon as a result of the Indian delegation's visit to Moscow amounted to only Rs. 95 million.[37] Most of the proposals were rejected by the Soviet experts on the grounds that the advantages claimed for them were either non-existent or marginal, or that the various estimates on which they were based were inaccurate, or that the savings in cost resulting from their adoption were nominal. Although the Soviets readily agreed that the proposed technologies for the melting shops and the slabbing mill were not the most advanced, they were unwilling to implement the advanced techniques – at least for the first stage of

Bokaro — on the grounds that these were in a trial stage in the Soviet Union.

Notes to Chapter 6

[1] *Cost Reduction Study on Bokaro Steel Project*, prepared by M. N. Dastur and Company, Private Ltd., May 19, 1966 (Calcutta). It is hereafter referred to as the *Cost Reduction Study*.

[2] This task was put on an emergency basis for reasons stated earlier on pp. 40-41.

[3] *Cost Reduction Study*, p. 5.1.

[4] Ibid., p. 2.2.

[5] Ibid., p. 12.

[6] Ibid., p. 13.

[7] Ibid., p. 13.

[8] *68th Report*, p. 25.

[9] Ibid., p. 26.

[10] *The Cost Reduction Study*, p. 16. 'This development enables liquid steel to be cast directly into slabs thus completely bypassing the heavy investments involved in conventional ingot teeming, pit-side facilities, stripper, soaking pits and slabbing mill. More important, the capital cost of continuous casting plant is considerably lower (only 50-60 percent that of slabbing mill facilities) and yield from steel to slab is about 10 percent higher, than by conventional methods proposed in the Soviet Report. In effect, operating costs (including fixed charges) are appreciably reduced.' Ibid., p. 2.43.

[11] Ibid.

[12] Ibid.

[13] The arguments of the Soviet technical team justifying the proposed slabbing mill design are reproduced at length in the *69th Report*, pp. 22-23.

[14] Iain M. D. Halliday, *Continuous Casting of Steel in the USSR — A Survey* (Organization for Economic Co-operation and Development, 1964). It is hereafter referred to as the *OECD Study*.

[15] Ibid., p. 60.

[16] *Cost Reduction Study*, pp. 2.5-2.6.

[17] Ibid., p. 2.10 for details.

[18] Ibid., p. 2.16.

[19] Ibid., p. 8.

[20] It was ultimately agreed that 90 percent of the estimated refractory requirements for the 1.7 million tonne stage would be met

from private Indian sources. However, by March 1970, the failure of
indigenous suppliers had necessitated the import of about 43,000
tonnes of refractories from the Soviet Union on an emergency basis,
thus raising the Soviet contribution to the total estimated refractory
requirements to 30 percent. For details, see pp. 74-75.

[21] *The Cost Reduction Study*, p. 29.

[22] Ibid., p. 30. The following interesting details throw some light
on the origins of this massive expenditure: 'For the Soviet specialists
Bokaro Steel would have to pay salaries (in Roubles) ranging from
Roubles 116 to 380 per month, together with an allowance ranging
from Rs. 44 to 83 per day, transfer allowance for specialists ranging
from Rs. 400 to 750, first-class air travel for specialist and his
familiy with up to 240 kg of baggage per family, first class air
travel on leave once in two years, hotel and travel between Delhi and
Bokaro on the way to Moscow and back, insurance, all business
travel within India, business trunk-calls and cables in India, cars, air
conditioned and furnished offices, air conditioned and fully-appoint-
ed accomodation, medical expenses including hospitalization, full
pay during sickness, provision of schools, clubs and excursion facilities etc., all free of taxes.' Ibid., pp. 2.156-2.157.

It is interesting that personnel from a socialist country insist on
first-class travel and air conditioned homes and clubs, inflating the
cost of the aid to an underdeveloped country much in the style and
practice of capitalist donor countries. It is equally ironic that the
average Soviet expert's standard of living in India exceeds his living
conditions in the Soviet Union; socialism does not go very far in
practice. The most unfortunate aspect of this phenomenon in the
case of Bokaro, however, was that a substantial amount of such
expenditure could have been avoided by the substitution of locally
available expertise.

Incidentally, the question of the salaries of Soviet specialists
working in public sector plants in India is continually debated in the
Indian Parliament. Indeed, it seemed to have strained the ability of
some Indian MPs at handling arithmetic. Thus, in April 1970, eleven
members of Parliament, all from the right-wing Swatantra Party,
wrote a letter to the Prime Minister stating that 940 Russian engineers had been paid an aggregate total salary of Rs. 125 million over
a period of three years. 'This way the per capita monthly salary of
Russian engineers amounts to an astronomical sum of about Rs.
35,000, i.e., 3½ times the salary of the President of India', the MPs
added. (*The Statesman* [Delhi], April 26, 1970.) Refuting their con-
tention, the Prime Minister said that, in terms of the information
supplied by the MPs themselves, the average monthly salary of the
Soviet technician worked out at Rs. 3,673 a month. 'Giving details

of the salaries paid to Russian technicians, Mrs. Gandhi said the highest paid persons were chief engineers in public sector steel plants who got Rs. 7,066 a month. The lowest paid Soviet technician received a salary of Rs. 2,633 a month.' (*The Statesman* [Delhi], May 6, 1970.)

A similar inaccuracy was corrected by K.C. Pant, Minister of State for Steel, in the Rajya Sabha. Replying to a question of whether there were over 500 Russian specialists at Bokaro, he said that there were actually only 159 Soviet specialists at Bokaro site as of January 31, 1970, although the agreement with the Soviet Union provided for the services of 572. (*The Times of India* [Delhi], March 17, 1970.)

[23] *The Cost Reduction Study*, p. 30.

[24] Ibid., p. 31.

[25] The contents of these two agreements with Dasturco are given on pp. 78-80.

[26] In this context, the modifications proposed by the Study in the massive slabbing mill and the Soviet reaction to them are discussed earlier on p. 55.

[27] *The Cost Reduction Study*, p. 17.

[28] For details, see the *68th Report*, p. 230.

[29] As a result of the discussions, the benzol recovery plant was deleted, the deletion resulting in savings of Rs. 25.7 million (ibid., p. 34).

[30] *The Cost Reduction Study*, p. 11. The suggested alternative of decentralizing foundry iron capacities was, however, not considered in any depth by the Study.

[31] *68th Report*, p. 40.

[32] Thus, the Study reported that during the expansion stage of Bhilai from a 1 million to 2.5 million tonne capacity, of the 29,296 men on its payroll in January 1964, 12,000 were for 'construction' purposes. (Ibid., p. 2.161.)

[33] Ibid., p. 2.167.

[34] Ibid., p. 4.1.

[35] Ibid., pp. 3.7-3.8.

[36] Ibid., p. 3.5.

[37] Dasturco was paid Rs. 850,000 for preparing the Cost Reduction Study.

CHAPTER 7

Current controversies on Bokaro

Bokaro became a domestic issue with the realization that Dasturco, an Indian firm of consulting engineers, was gradually being displaced from its dominating role as designer and builder of the steel mill because of Soviet collaboration. The controversy over Bokaro evolved to include such issues as the 'economics' of the project in terms of its prospective profitability, revisions in the estimates of the project, delays in its construction and commissioning, etc. Bokaro's problems, as its construction was initiated in 1967, were increasingly attributed to Soviet aid-financing.

The political aspect of the controversy is underlined by questions raised in the Indian Parliament. The right-wing Jan Sangh and Swatantra Parties — and, recently, the Organization Congress Party — are explicitly anti-Soviet in their inquiries. They question whether the CEDB (a Government of India agency), rather than Dasturco, was assigned the role of primary consultant in the design contract for Bokaro's expansion to 4 million tonne capacity under Soviet pressure; whether the Soviet specialists on the Bokaro site demonstrated an 'overbearing' attitude; and whether Mr. S.A. Dange, the leader of the Soviet-oriented Communist Party of India, was up for appointment as

director of Hindustan Steel Ltd. Such queries are obvious-
ly anti-Soviet, in both content and intention.[1]

The second aspect of the controversy concentrates on
such issues as the revisions in the schedules and cost estimates for Bokaro that arise, for the most part, from various kinds of delays, and the high cost estimates of Bokaro's output. Such considerations lead to the argument that
it was futile to concentrate resources in such a massive
project.[2] Some of these attitudes arise from a desire for
'self-reliance for India', some from opposition to the public sector and the bureaucracy (the former is generally
thought to be wasteful and the latter high-handed). Consequently, they are pro-Dastur and, thus, anti-Soviet.

In the final category are Dastur's own comments on the
issues under discussion, especially on the displacement of
Dasturco as consultants and engineers for the steel plant.[3]
According to Dastur's judgment, the replacement of Dasturco's extensive services is a special case of the general
phenomenon of indiscriminate import by India of technology and services from foreign sources, in both the public
and private sectors and across industries. The reasons for
this phenomenon are traced first to the fact that 'general-
ist-bureaucrats' make decisions on imports of technology
without having the competence to undertake an effective
scrutiny of such imports and, second, to the pressures
exercised by donor countries which are not resisted effectively by recipient countries anxious to secure aid.

These controversies should be judged in the light of
available facts. First is the issue of the revision in the estimates of the project, by now a well-known and general
feature of project planning in India. The estimate announced in March 1970 of Rs. 7.6 billion with a foreign exchange component of Rs. 1.95 billion for the first stage of
1.7 million tonnes exceeded the original estimate by
Rs. 900 million. This increase was explained in terms of an
estimated rise in the supply prices of *indigenous* equipment, accounting for Rs. 600 million. The remainder was

accounted for by a rise in the price of steel and wages.[4]

Next we analyze the reasons for the postponement of the construction and commissioning schedule of Bokaro. The latest schedule announced in February 1969 postponed the commissioning of the first blast furnace to March 1972, and of the entire first stage to June 1973. This indicates a delay of 27 months in the initial schedule prepared in November 1966.

The reasons for the postponement of the construction schedule of Bokaro can be traced to delays in the supplies of working drawings, equipment, structurals and materials from various sources. The sources of supplies of the various items and the delays under each category are presented in Tables 1 and 2. Table 1 puts the estimated supplies of equipment, structurals and refractories from the Soviet Union, for the first stage of Bokaro, at 37 percent, 9 percent, and 10 percent respectively. It is clear from Table 2 that the backlogs in the scheduled supplies from the various sources do not show striking differences in performance. With respect to the supplies of equipment and structurals, private suppliers in India and the MAMC in the public sector show the worst performance; while the former are handicapped by the non-availability of steel and imported components, the latter is plagued with a special set of problems. Again, while the Soviet Union and the HEC indicate better performance in terms of the amounts of equipment supplied by a certain date, both these indicators of performance are nominal rather than real. In the case of the Soviet Union, the contract specified that the items of equipment could be supplied within a period of fifty months from the date of signing of the contract, without any specifications relating to the phasing of the deliveries. In the case of the HEC, the entire schedule was revised to suit its manufacturing potential. The delays by the HEC are attributed largely to its gigantic organizational deficiencies.

The controversies relating to the 'worthwhileness' of

TABLE 1

Sources of Equipment, Structurals and Refractories for Bokaro:
Stage I[1]

Item (1)	Total to be supplied (in tonnes) (2)	Source of supply (3)	Proportion to be supplied by (3) (4)
A. Equipment	276,795	(a) USSR and Czechoslovakia	37
		(b) Indian plublic sector, including workshops of Bokaro Steel Limited	41
		(c) Indian private sector	22
B. Structurals	239,576	(a) USSR	9
		(b) Indian public sector	73
		(c) Indian private sector	18
C. Refractories	212,087	(a) USSR	10
		(b) Indian private sector	90

[1] The Table is derived from information given in the *68th Report*, pp. 43-44.

Bokaro should also be judged in the light of the available factual evidence. These are based on extremely limited indicators. Two typical attempts at such evaluation are considered below.

The first, based on Table 3, relates to comparisons, in terms of plant cost per annual ingot ton, of comparable steelworks in Japan, Italy, and England. Table 3 indicates that it would have been possible during 1962-1966 to design and install elsewhere a steelworks with a capacity of 1.7 million tons at a plant cost of between Rs. 1,500-2,000 million. The comparable cost for Bokaro in India would be

TABLE 2

Performance in Terms of Scheduling of Targeted Supplies by Various
Suppliers

Item (1)	Source of supply (2)	Amount to be supplied (in tonnes) (3)	Amount actually supplied (in percent) (4)	Target date (5)
Design Documentation	USSR	93,000 (total under contract)	98 (supplied within 24 months of signing of contract)	Not specified
Equipment	USSR	101,502	69 Received by the end	The contract for the supply of
Steel Structurals	USSR	21,443	39 of January, 1970	equipment specified that all items of equipment
Refractories	USSR	23,138[1]	Not given	would be supplied within a period of
Pipes and Other Goods	USSR	23,929	Not given	50 months from the date of signing of the contract, i.e., by July 31, 1970. The contract did not specify a phased delivery schedule.
Equipment	HEC[2]	72,000	57 (As of January,	December, 1971
Steel Structurals	HEC	27,210	87 1970)	December, 1971
Equipment	MAMC[3]	4,650	15 (As of February 25, 1970)	By the first quarter of 1970
Equipment	Indian[4] private sector	14,737	23	Not specified
Steel Structurals		3,349	31	Not specified

Item (1)	Source of supply (2)	Amount to be supplied (in tonnes) (3)	Amount actually supplied (in percent) (4)	Target date (5)
Cranes[5]	...	Total 351 units of which	11 (of the targeted supplies of 210 cranes by the first quarter of 1970)	By the first quarter of 1970
	USSR	8 percent		
	Indian public sector	31 percent		
	Indian private sector	61 percent		
Refractories	Indian private sector[6]	162,888 tonnes	8 (received till the end of January, 1970)	Not specified
	USSR	4,791 tonnes	48	

[1] The contract for the supply of 18,347 tonnes of refractories was finalized on July 9, 1969.

[2] The information on HEC is from a revised schedule finalized in November 1968, since the earlier delivery schedule of June 30, 1967 was prepared by Bokaro Steel Limited, taking into account its own construction schedule and not HEC's manufacturing capability. Incidentally, the HEC did not supply the equipment in the desired sequence.

[3] The information on MAMC is according to the schedule revised in July 1969 at MAMC's request. The Committee on Public Undertakings expressed the view that the MAMC would not be able to make the supplies according to its commitments. Therefore, the Committee suggested that Bokaro Steel Limited arrange for alternative sources of supply in order to ensure that its own construction schedule would not be disturbed on account of the failure of MAMC to meet its commitments.

[4] The private sector suppliers gave as reasons for the delay the non-availability of steel and imported components.

[5] The position with respect to the supply of cranes was described as precarious by the *68th Report*.

[6] Due to the failure of indigenous suppliers, an additional import of 18,000 tonnes of refractories was ordered from the USSR in December 1969. A further import of 25,025 tonnes of refractories from the USSR is also to be ordered shortly to avoid disturbing the construction schedule of Bokaro (see *68th Report*, p. 51). One of the many reasons advanced by the Indian manufacturers for the delay was the stringent specifications of the refractories by the Soviet agencies. Thus, informing the Committee on Public Undertakings of the high rejections of their bricks on the basis of visual inspection, the representatives of the Indian Refractory Makers Association stated:

> We were greatly surprised to know that the Russian experts were not satisfied with the looks of the bricks. For the first time, we had that experience. No German expert, no American expert, no British expert even discussed the looks of bricks. These bricks were meant for constructing furnaces, not for architectural buildings. The chemical and physical properties were all right and they were completely satisfactory. We were taken by surprise when the bricks were rejected on the ground of looks. (*68th Report*, p. 53.)

Rs. 4,862 million. Bokaro, however, cannot be built at a low cost in India for three reasons. In the first place, the costs of basic construction materials such as cement and structurals, as well as reinforcing steel, are higher in India than, say, in Japan. The structural and civil work constitutes about 25 to 30 percent of total plant cost. Second, the cost of equipment manufactured in India is likely to be higher than in other countries with a long fabricating experience. Finally, the plant cost per annual ingot tonne for Bokaro's 1.7 million tonne stage gets pushed up on account of the fixed investment costs, incorporated from Stage I itself for the eventual expansion to the 5.5 million tonne capacity. Apparently for these reasons, the plant cost per annual ingot tonne of Indian steel plants is consistently higher than those of steel plants abroad.[5]

TABLE 3

Plant Cost per Annual Ingot Ton for Comparable Steelworks

Steelworks (1)	Year of completion (2)	Initial ingot steel capacity (million tons/ year) (3)	Mill complex (4)	Plant cost per annu- al ingot ton[1] (5)
Fukuyama	1966	1.50	46″ Universal slabbing mill 80″ Continuous hot strip mill 80″ 5 stand tan- dem cold mill	Rs. 992
Spencer Works (U.K.)	1962	1.40	45″ Universal slabbing mill 68″ Continuous hot strip mill 68″ 4 stand tan- dem cold mill	Rs. 1,170
Taranto (Italy)	1964	2.50	46″ Universal slabbing mill 68″ Continuous hot strip mill 140″ Plate mill, pipe plant	Rs. , 861
Bokaro	Stage 1	1.70	50″ Universal slabbing mill	Rs. 2,860

80″ Continuous hot strip mill
80″ 4 stand tandem cold mill

Source: Dasturco, *Cost Reduction Study,* Table 5.1, p. 5.4.

[1] Plant cost excludes customs duty, costs of township, offsite facilities, designing and engineering.

A second attempt at judging Bokaro's worthwhileness is in terms of relating the costs of some of the outputs with comparable alternatives. These are presented in Table 4.

These cost comparisons, limited as they are, cannot be regarded as indicating the economics of Bokaro, especially at the 4 million tonne capacity, in a favorable or unfavorable light. In any case, simple arithmetical associations of scale and costs[6] bypass considerations of the managerial and organizational limitations affecting the operation of steel plants in India.[7]

Finally, the one controversial issue that can be genuinely substantiated by facts is the ouster of Dasturco as primary consultant for Bokaro. The fact that it was gradually eased out from its dominating role as designer and engineer of the steel plant is brought out by the contrasts in the two successive agreements signed with the firm. According to the initial agreement signed with Dasturco in April 1964, the scope of its consulting and engineering services included:

TABLE 4

Costs of Production in Rupees per Tonne of Bokaro (Estimated) and
Rourkela (Actual) Outputs

	Rourkela	Bokaro		
		Current Estimates of Steel Ministry		Estimates[1] indicated by the Soviet DPR at 4 million tonne stage
Item (1)	Actuals for 1968-1969 (2)	1.7 million tonne stage (3)	4 million tonne stage (4)	(5)
Pig iron	347.53	379	277	151 (Basic iron) 163 (Foundry)
Steel ingots	411.15	629	424	224
Hot rolled coils	647.63	860[2]	586[2]	345[2]
Hot rolled sheets	701.24	—	—	—
Cold rolled sheets	1111.93	1100[2]	743[2]	437[2]

Source: *68th Report,* pp. 69-70, 72.

[1] These estimates in the Soviet Detailed Project Report (DPR) do not include interest on capital, cost of offsite facilities, cost of engineering, technical supervision and administration during construction, customs duties, taxes, etc. They are also based on raw material prices prevailing in 1964. Current estimates of the Steel Ministry for Bokaro presumably include the former charges.

[2] Figures refer to costs of sheets and coils.

(1) preparing the general layout of the plant;
(2) preparing the layout of each main and ancillary department with details of the required machinery;
(3) advising Bokaro Steel Ltd. on the planning of all the required preliminary work at the site;

(4) preparing an overall schedule for constructing and erecting the plant and other facilities;

(5) preparing documents for inviting tenders of machinery and equipment, scrutinizing these, and recommending the suppliers with suitable offers;

(6) preparing all the drawings required for the establishment of the plant;

(7) supervising all construction and erection;

(8) arranging the guarantee tests for the different units of the plant;

(9) arranging the guarantee tests for the integrated operation of the plant; and

(10) demonstrating within a period of 18 months of the commissioning of the last unit of the plant that it will 'have the full capacity at the rated annual output'.

The second agreement, signed on February 25, 1967 after finalizing Soviet collaboration, specified Dasturco's functions as:

(1) preparing and submitting tender documents for plant *equipment and machinery* which are 'outside the scope of supplies of Soviet suppliers' and are to be procured from the Indian private sector, scrutinizing these and advising Bokaro Steel Ltd. on the suitability of the offers;

(2) preparing and submitting tender documents for the construction and erection services to be contracted out to agencies other than the Indian public sector, scrutinizing these, and recommending their acceptance;

(3) inspecting equipment procured from sources other than the Soviet suppliers and the Indian public sector;

(4) preparing the drawings for those units of the plant which are not to be supplied by the Soviet consultants; and

(5) submitting specifications of equipment and providing

designers' supervision for the units assigned to Dasturco.

It is clear that while, in the initial agreement, Dasturco was assigned the entire job of setting up Bokaro, from preparing the site and designing the plant with all the drawings and specifications, supervising and scheduling its construction, inviting *all* the tenders, and guaranteeing its operation, in the second agreement its role was reduced to preparing and inviting tenders for equipment and some services from the Indian private sector, and designing the equipment and providing designers' supervision for the units of the plant assigned to the firm. Indeed, the reversal of Dasturco's role is so obvious that one cannot but sympathize with its predicament, even when the reasons for the reversal are not analyzed in depth and the arguments underlying it are stated in terms of 'Soviet pressures', 'capitulation of the Indian bureaucracy to these' and so on. The more compelling reasons for Dasturco's displacement are analyzed earlier on pp. 41-46, in terms of the constraints imposed on the course of the negotiations by the policy objectives relating to the steel industry in India. Indeed, it was the combination of all these pervasive Goliath-sized factors which reduced Dasturco to the role of an unfortunate, but rather tenacious, David.

Notes to Chapter 7

[1] See, for example, the reports of these debates in the *Times of India* (Delhi), March 17 and April 23, 1970, and the *Statesman* (Delhi), April 23 and April 30, 1970. See also p. 66 above for a letter from several Swatantra Party MPs to the Prime Minister inquiring if Soviet specialists in India were receiving 'astronomical' salaries. The letter also singled out losses in Soviet-aided projects, thereby implying that this phenomenon was restricted to these enterprises.

[2] See 'What Is Ailing Bokaro?', *Indian Express* (Bombay), July 12, 1970; Virendra Agarwal, 'Bokaro — A White Elephant', *Indian*

Express, July 7, 1970; and K.V. Subrahmanyam, 'The Tragedy of Bokaro', *Economic Times* (Bombay), February 4, 1970. See the following letters to the editor: N.P. Viswam, 'Big Brother and Bokaro', *Statesman* (Delhi); and K.V. Subrahmanyam, 'Bokaro Delays — Specious Excuses', *Hindustan Times* (Delhi), February 23, 1970. See also 'Closing the Options in Steel', *Economic and Political Weekly*, February 28, 1970.

[3] These are expressed in two articles: 'Collaboration at India's Cost', *Citizen* (Delhi), April 11, 1970 and 'Implications', *Seminar* (Delhi), July 13, 1970 on 'Foreign Technology: A Symposium on Its Role in our Future Development'.

[4] For details, see the *68th Report*, pp. 51-59.

[5] The high plant investment costs per tonne in Indian steel plants are sometimes attributed to the inability to bid in world markets for equipment purchases because of aid-tying (see, for example, a report in the *Statesman* [Delhi] April 26, 1968). Ideally, one could work out the direct costs of aid-tying by estimating the excess of the costs of importing a given package of equipment and services from the donor country over the costs of importing the *same* package from the cheapest available source. Such a comparison of the costs of aid-tying between two sources of aid would have to make allowances for differences in the terms and conditions of aid and the quality of equipment supplied, etc. If this argument is applied concretely to Bokaro, it would be difficult to say if the costs of tying the purchases of equipment and services for the project as worked out in the Soviet Project Report to, say, American sources would have been less than the costs of having to acquire them from Soviet sources. There is no conclusive evidence that Soviet equipment prices are higher.

It is, however, quite possible that the *total* plant cost per tonne would be higher under the present arrangement with the Soviet Union with a lower foreign exchange component than under an alternative arrangement with American collaboration with a higher foreign exchange cost. In the current arrangement with Soviet collaboration, with larger possibilities of import substitution, the total plant unit cost would be higher because the domestic prices of equipment and materials are higher all along the line and the dislocations in construction arising from delayed domestic supplies push up costs further. Thus, while import substitution in building a steel plant can be pursued as an end in itself, it does not necessarily result in a cheap and efficient steel plant. Apart from steel plant costs, what is of crucial relevance under this strategy is the possibility that with a basic domestic supplier such as the HEC continuously in the red, the entire steel program of an additional one million tonne steel capacity per annum in the seventies may be seriously jeopardized.

[6] This applies also to the comparisons in Table 3.

[7] Calculations of the "worthwhileness" of Bokaro in terms of cost-benefit analysis can be pursued at various levels of depth. From the analytical point of view, it is necessary to distinguish among at least three aspects of such calculations. The question of whether India should produce steel at all could be answered in terms of the rate of return that a steel plant would earn in India under certain 'non-distortionary' assumptions with respect to prices of raw materials and final products, scale and composition of the outputs, the foreign exchange rate, and so on. Thus, it is estimated that with no 'distortions' in the system, an optimal-sized steel plant in India could earn a rate of return of 14 to 17 percent (see William Johnson, The Steel Industry in India [Harvard University Press, 1966]). The rate of return from Bokaro, as designed by the U.S. Steel Report, with the outputs valued at market prices was estimated to be over 20 percent before taxes. Such calculations, therefore, would yield definitive arguments about whether a steel plant with corresponding features should be established in India.

However, in actual practice, the rate of return diverges from the optimum because of two sets of factors. In the first place, non-economic objectives such as regional dispersal of industries or the decision to prevent concentration of monopoly power would affect the location and size of a project and, hence, its returns. However, when such divergences arise from the rational pursuit of these non-economic objectives they should be identified, if possible quantificated, and strongly defended in terms of second-best arguments that derive their rationale from non-economic objectives.

However, the divergences from the optimum rate of return which cannot be defended are those that arise from non-justifiable distortions in the entire system or in the plant itself. These may be due to wrong pricing of some material or from organizational-*cum*-managerial limitations. These factors, too, must be identified, systematically tabulated, and persistently tackled over a length of time, with periodic indications about their trend of performance. For example, it would be very instructive to find out if, during the brief history of the three steel plants in the public sector, the iron ore consumption per unit of ingot steel is declining, if the quality of the outputs is improving in terms of some well-defined norms, if the technical performance of the machines or sections of the plants is steadily improving over time. Such detailed physical-*cum*-technical trends give a more definite idea of the plant's ultimate potential for good performance.

In current discussions and defense of public-sector steel plant performance, an analytical framework that would provide rational arguments for judging its record is generally absent. Instead, the endless apologia on losses which are attributed to high interest and depreciation charges on the capital blocked in massive built-in capacities, and to costs of townships, etc., merely sidetrack the real issues. What is more crucial is that there should be a genuine consolidation in the physical-*cum*-technical criteria of performance (suggested above) so that when the plants reach their break-even points, they are well-entrenched to make profits.

CHAPTER 8

The lessons and conclusions

Several conclusions emerge from the foregoing analysis.

(A) For the Indian steel industry, the lessons of Bokaro are related to the objectives it was supposed to fulfill.[1] As indicated in the Planning Commission Note on Bokaro, these were:

(1) It must be a 'cheap' plant;
(2) It must have an advanced technology;
(3) It must provide the maximum opportunities for import substitution, especially in consulting services;
(4) Its import requirements should be financed by foreign aid arrangement; and
(5) It must be designed, engineered, and managed by local skills and expertise.

No conceivable arrangement could have guaranteed the fulfillment of all the objectives simultaneously. In particular, Bokaro illustrates the conflict between (1) and (3), between (2) and (4), between (3) and (4) and between (4) and (5). It is clear that while the expansion of steel in the public sector is assigned a high priority in the Indian planning process, the expansion program is loaded with too many conflicting constraints and no clear-cut indication about which one is dispensable.

The analysis reveals that arranging for Bokaro's import requirements with aid-financing from *any* source would necessarily imply, as it did with Soviet aid, that India would retain no initiative in bargaining for the crucial details of the arrangement. Given the aid-tying practices of donor-countries, it was inevitable that the Soviet Union, which was treated as the lender of the last resort, would end up by tying supplies of equipment to consulting services and complete control over the management of its construction during the first phase.[2] With no Indian bargaining maneuverability arising from the possibility of an alternative source of foreign funds, it was inevitable that the Soviet negotiators refused to consider significant reductions in the cost estimates of the project and went ahead with the adoption of second-best technology for the steel melting shops and the slabbing mill. One would hesitate to regard the activation of the heavy engineering capacities in the Indian public sector for the supply of Bokaro requirements as a net gain in import substitution under the Soviet aid-arrangement. The fact that these capacities were Soviet-aided was a sufficient incentive for the Soviet Union to keep them efficiently utilized.

If it was thought that Bokaro could have been designed, engineered, and supervised during its construction by the Indian consulting and engineering firm of Dastur and Company, with heavy reliance on supplies of equipment, structurals, refractories, and technical skill from Indian sources, the pursuit of these objectives, as set forth in the Planning Commission Note on Bokaro, under any aid-financed arrangement for the plant's import requirements was bound to alter its crucial features. It is surprising that the alternative of financing the plant's foreign exchange requirements, preferably with suppliers' credits or even with free foreign exchange at the rate of about 45 to 64 million dollars per year during its construction, was not seriously considered.

It would, therefore, seem that the fact of the Soviet Union ultimately executing Bokaro as a turn-key job under Soviet aid-financing was the result of the lack of a policy framework relating to the steel industry, and especially of inadequate foreign exchange planning in general. The pressure-*cum*-conspiracy hypothesis that seeks to explain Dasturco's ouster in terms of an unwitting or deliberate 'capitulation' of the Indian negotiators in the steel ministry to 'pressures' exercised by the Soviet negotiators is simplistic. It is to be hoped that in the planning of future steel capacities in India, the lessons learned at some cost from Bokaro will be applied: total reliance on aid from any source for financing the foreign exchange requirements of additional steel plants, or indeed any major projects, is bound to result in the sacrifice, as in the case of Bokaro, of national objectives such as technological self-reliance.

(B) There are lessons from Bokaro also for the Soviet Union. There is no doubt that the continuous debate on Bokaro in India arose out of the phenomenon of an Indian consulting firm being gradually edged out of its predominant role as consultants and designers of the steel plant. The debate on this issue has remained animated and detrimental to the Soviet image in India; indeed, given the current climate of self-reliance, criticism of the Soviet Union cuts across party lines. In view of this, the 'returns' to the Soviet Union on aid to Bokaro are unlikely to match those arising from its aid participation in the Indian oil industry. In the latter case, technical expertise in oil exploration was acquired from Soviet (and East European) sources with an overwhelming sense of gratitude in view of the indigenous weakness in knowhow vis-a-vis the Western oil monopolies. Indeed, unless the Soviet Union comes to grips with the fact of a vastly increased technological competence and a growing stress on technological self-reliance in India, the future of Indo-Soviet economic collaboration is likely to be bleak and the Bokaro episode more than a temporary lapse in Soviet aid diplomacy.

Notes to Chapter 8

[1] As already argued earlier, the basic objective of import-substituting in steel in India is fully defensible on economic grounds.

[2] Indeed, as argued at length earlier, there is ample evidence to suggest that, in a possible aid arrangement with the United States, the U.S. Steel Corporation would also have removed Dastur and Company from its role as primary consultants and undertaken the steel mill's construction only on a turn-key basis.

Chronology of events relating to the Indo-Soviet collaboration in the Bokaro steel plant

Date and Year (1)	Details of Meeting or Agreement (2)	Dr. Dastur's Comments (3)
July 1964	An Indian delegation was sent to Moscow for holding discussions with a Soviet team. During these discussions, it was agreed that 'a Soviet Technical Team would visit India for detailed discussions with the Consultants [Dasturco] on the project' (*68th* Report of the C.P.U., p. 11)	The absence of a 'clear stand' at the meetings encouraged the Soviets 'to dictate terms later on' (Ibid., p. 11)
August 1964	Technical discussions on the project between the representatives of the two governments in Delhi.	'To its surprise, Dasturco was completely kept out of the discussions with the Soviet Team which visited India in August, 1964. It was unfortunate that Dasturco was not associated with any of the technical discussions with the Soviets thereafter which had important technical implications and ultimately resulted in a high cost project' (Ibid., p. 11)

Comments of the Representative of the Steel Ministry (4)	Comments of the *68th Report* of the C.P.U. (5)
'Dr. Dastur was part of delegation to Moscow. The whole object was to see how much of the Consultancy we would get for Dasturco. We discussed it for several days and unfortunately we were not able to persuade the Soviets to give a large chunk to Dasturco' (Ibid., p. 15)	'The important point was not to secure enough work for Dasturco, but it was far more important that Dasturco's knowledge and experience ought to have been fully utilized for the establishment of a technically sound and economic steel project to suit the Indian conditions. The whole purpose of getting the design consultancy set up by Dasturco with the Government initiative at the earlier stages was lost sight of and it was not put to good use in setting up the Bokaro Steel Plant for which purpose alone Dasturco was brought to India' (Ibid., p. 16)
'... it was more or less settled at that time [July 1964] as to what exactly the Dasturco will be getting. Then the August 1964 meeting was mainly for the purpose of settling certain details and the fact finding mission came from USSR and it was not felt necessary to ask Dastur to associate with that Mission' (Ibid., p. 15)	The Committee was distressed that 'Dasturco who were the General Consultant of the Ministry were completely sidetracked while technical details were settled for the drawing up of the D.P.R. [Detailed Project Report] for Bokaro Steel Project' (Ibid., p. 16)

Date and Year (1)	Details of Meeting or Agreement (2)	Dr. Dastur's Comments (3)
January 25, 1965	An Agreement was signed between the Government of India and the Government of the USSR for financial aid and technical collaboration for establishing the Bokaro Steel Mill. The Soviet Government also extended a credit of up to 200 million roubles (or Rs. 1,666 million at post-devaluation exchange rates) for meeting the foreign exchange cost of the plant bearing an interest rate of 2.5 percent and repayable in twelve years.	
February 5, 1965	Signing of a contract between the representatives of Tiazpromexport and the Bokaro Steel Limited for the preparation and submission of a Detailed Project Report to suit Soviet technology and equipment.	

Comments of the Representative of the Steel Ministry (4)	Comments of the *68th Report* of the C.P.U. (5)

Date and Year (1)	Details of Meeting or Agreement (2)	Dr. Dastur's Comments (3)
December 22, 1965	The Detailed Project Report was submitted by Tiazpromexport and was examined by a Technical Committee of the Government of India consisting of 22 members of which two members represented Dasturco and two The Tata Iron & Steel Company.	Dr. Dastur doubted both the competence of the Technical Committee and the time allotted to it for the task of scrutinizing the Soviet Detailed Project Report consisting of 28 volumes. 'However, the purpose was just to show that there was a committee appointed and have a front' (Ibid., p. 12)
January 1966	Submission of the Technical Committee's Report on the Soviet D.P.R.	
March 29, 1966	Acceptance of the Soviet Detailed Project Report by the Government of India. The Memorandum of Acceptance of the D.P.R. provided that the Soviet consultants would give due consideration to concrete technical suggestions for cost reduction which might be made to them by the Indian side within three months.	

Comments of the Representative of the Steel Ministry (4)	Comments of the *68th Report* of the C.P.U. (5)
	'The Committee feel that the D.P.R. [Detailed Project Report] deserved a far greater scrutiny and that it was not given a proper technical appraisal on the basis of which investment decision of over Rs. 600 crores ought to have been made' (Ibid., p. 16)
	'The Government ought to have insisted on having enough time for the consideration of the report and other connected matters before signing the agreement' (Ibid., p. 29)

Date and Year (1)	Details of Meeting or Agreement (2)	Dr. Dastur's Comments (3)
March 29, 1966	The Ministry of Steel requested Dasturco to suggest concrete proposals for cost reduction *within seven weeks.*	'During the very limited time (seven weeks) available only major items of reduction are indicated. Further scope for cost reduction exists and could be realised by continuing study and implementation during engineering and construction of the plant.' (Ibid., p. 19)
May 21, 1966	Submission of the Cost Reduction Study by Dasturco.	'The Soviet proposals on technology and equipment are retained as far as possible. Changes are suggested only where the resulting benefits are substantial, where the modifications will also fully meet the requirements for efficient plant operations and where they are feasible at this stage and will not delay construction' (Ibid., p. 19)

Comments of the Representative of the Steel Ministry (4)	Comments of the *68th Report* of the C.P.U. (5)
	'Dasturco was also asked to make a cost reduction study after signing the Memorandum on the acceptance of the D.P.R. The Committee, however, feel that this ought to have been done before signing the Memorandum of acceptance. It was explained to the Committee that the agreement had to be signed within two months of the submission of the D.P.R. The Committee feel that the government should have resisted being stampeded into signing such an important agreement without a proper and detailed scrutiny' (Ibid., p. 17)
'The Cost Reduction Study Report submitted by Dasturco on 21st May, 1966 lacked detailed technical design basis, detailed cost calculations and break-up of cost savings. It was not, therefore, possible for BSL [Bokaro Steel Ltd.] to assess the quantum of savings given in the cost reduction study. This was necessary to analyse the technical acceptability of the suggestion and also to judge as to what extent the savings estimated by Dasturco were realistic... .' (Ibid., p. 20)	

Date and Year (1)	Details of Meeting or Agreement (2)	Dr. Dastur's Comments (3)
May 3, 1966	Signing of an Agreement with Tiazpromexport for the supply of equipment and materials from the USSR, rendering of technical assistance in the construction and erection of the plant and deputation of Soviet specialists to Bokaro for that purpose. Another agreement was also signed for the supply of working drawings.	
May 28, 1966	Meeting between the representatives of the Bokaro Steel Limited and Dasturco at which Dasturco were requested to furnish detailed breakdown of the possible savings in the estimates of the Soviet Detailed Project Report (Ibid., p. 20)	
June 4, 1966	Meeting between the representatives of the Bokaro Steel Limited and Dasturco during which the latter indicated that they had not worked out the detailed figures of possible savings because 'they did not clearly understand what Bokaro Steel Ltd. wanted' (Ibid., p. 20)	

Comments of the Representative of the Steel Ministry (4)	Comments of the *68th Report* of the C.P.U. (5)
'... Bokaro Steel Ltd., made its best efforts to get the details of the cost reduction proposals. But in spite of the best efforts to secure this information during the course of two weeks' discussion they had with M/s. Dasturco at Calcutta, they failed to secure the required information. They submitted their interim comments on 16th June, 1966, pending receipt of details from Dasturco' (Ibid., p. 20)	'The Committee feel that all the discussions with Dasturco ought to have taken place in India and all the points should have been sorted out before going to Moscow' (Ibid., p. 29)

Date and Year (1)	Details of Meeting or Agreement (2)	Dr. Dastur's Comments (3)
	'Dasturco promised to try and give this information during the course of the week' (Ibid., p. 20)	
June 7, 1966	Meeting among the representatives of Bokaro Steel Ltd., Dasturco, the Planning Commission and the Ministry of Finance. The purpose of the meeting was to work out suitable instructions for the Indian delegation on the various points covered by the Cost Reduction Study. During the meeting, the Chairman, Bokaro Steel Ltd. informed the members that 'the Study as presented did not give a break-up of the savings... .' (Ibid., p. 20)	
	Dasturco, however, gave an assurance that 'the working sheets containing details will be put up before the Soviet Consultants at Moscow' (Ibid., p. 20)	

Comments of the Representative of the Steel Ministry (4)	Comments of the *68th Report* of the C.P.U. (5)

Date and Year (1)	Details of Meeting or Agreement (2)	Dr. Dastur's Comments (3)
June 1966	Discussions in Moscow between the Indian delegation, of which 10 members were representatives of Dasturco, and the Soviet delegation on Dasturco's proposals for cost reduction. 'The Soviet side expressed the view that Dasturco's recommendations for the reduction of equipment and cost were unrealistic and technically unacceptable in most cases. Against a reduction of Rs. 1,075 million recommended by Dasturco, the net reduction as a result of the delegation's visit to Moscow amounted to Rs. 95 million only' (Ibid., p. 21)	During his evidence before the Committee, Dr. Dastur stated that 'in the discussions held in Moscow, the Chairman, Bokaro Steel Ltd., dominated in the meetings. Whereas from the Soviet side, the head of Design Institute, my equivalent was the leader of their team and he used to argue, from our side Mr. Wanchoo was the leader of our team and he used to argue and we were only allowed to have a few words in sideways' (Ibid., p. 26)

Comments of the Representative of the Steel Ministry (4)	Comments of the *68th Report* of the C.P.U. (5)
Mr. Wanchoo, the Chairman of Bokaro Steel Limited, stated during his evidence before the Committee: 'I certainly led the Delegation. We had about a dozen technicians including Dastur, Hindustan Steel Design Bureau and Bokaro Managing Director, who himself was a technician. I felt that in the opening session of this conference — the conference went on for two to three weeks — I should be the principal speaker, and therefore, I presented to the other side the case which was Dastur's case, our case, Bokaro's case and the Government of India's case. I presented the case on behalf of the Government of India. They naturally had some technicians and they presented their case. Obviously, we could not discuss the technical details in the main conference of this nature. So, what was decided was that we appointed 5 or 6 panels, consisting wholly of technicians in each of which Dastur was represented. These panels were to discuss technical matters in detail.... At the end, all the panels reported their agreements or disagreements to the main Committee, of which again I was the Chairman. So I took the leading part on the first day when we were starting the discussion, and again on the last day. In fact, I was not present even in the panels, not	'The Committee also feel that it would have been better if the leader of the delegation which was to discuss highly technical matters had been a technical person especially when on the other side, the head of the team was a technical man. They desire that the delegations for such technical negotiations either with foreign companies or Governments should as far as possible be headed by technical chiefs' (Ibid., p. 29)

'The Committee are left with the impression that there was lack of cooperation and proper understanding among M/s. Dasturco, Bokaro Steel Plant and the Government of India. Had there been a greater understanding and cooperation, probably the results would have been better in the interest of the country' (Ibid., p. 29) |

Date and Year (1)	Details of Meeting or Agreement (2)	Dr. Dastur's Comments (3)
January 25, 1967	A contract was signed with Dasturco under which they were engaged to work as Indian consulting engineers on the 1.7 million tonne stage of Bokaro for a period of seven years for a fee of Rs. 18.35 million.	'... originally the Company was supposed to handle complete engineering work on Bokaro Steel but after the agreement with USSR the major part of the work was taken out of the hands of the company and they were assigned a minor role in the Bokaro Project' (Ibid., p. 13)

Comments of the Representative of the Steel Ministry (4)	Comments of the *68th Report* of the C.P.U. (5)

being a technician myself. But I felt it necessary to present the Government of India's case fully myself on the first day, and of course, to take part on the last day' (Ibid., pp. 26-27)

'Dr. Dastur wanted to be the principal consultant for the project. The Soviet authorities who gave 200 million Roubles were not willing to accept this. They said this to the Minister, to me and they said this at all levels. They said that they must remain in full final authority of the project although they would associate with Dasturco' (Ibid., p. 15)

'The Committee feel that the Chairman of B.S.L. [Bokaro Steel Limited] who was also the Secretary of the Steel Ministry at the time reversed the whole position of Dasturco as a principal steel consultant as was reported to the Lok Sabha on 9th April, 1964' (Ibid., p. 16)

The Central Engineering and Design Bureau (CEDB) and the Hindustan Steel Construction Limited (HSCL)

(1) The CEDB began with a nucleus of 13 engineers in 1959. In February 1970, it was reported to have a staff of over 400 engineers, architects, metallurgists and town planners. Within a decade of its establishment, the CEDB had undertaken consulting work on designing projects with a value of Rs. 3,000 million. The consulting jobs for the expansion of the Rourkela plant capacity from 1.6 million tonnes to 1.8 million tonnes (completed in 1969) and of the Durgapur plant from 1.2 million tonnes to 1.6 million tonnes (completed in 1968) was done by the CEDB. It is currently reported to be handling 13 major projects, commissioned mainly by the State governments.

The extension of the activities of the CEDB to include designing of steel plant equipment in addition to preparing project reports was initiated with the agreements signed with the United Engineering and Foundry Company of America and C. Otto of Germany. The agreement with Gipromez of the Soviet Union followed in early 1970. (For more details, see the article titled 'HSL Revamps its Design Bureau' by U.N. Phadnis in the *Hindustan Times* [Delhi], February 9, 1970). The CEDB was also reported considering an agreement with Voest of Austria (*The*

Times of India [Delhi], April 19, 1970). It would, there-fore, seem that the CEDB had been consolidating its technical repertoire through agreements with various sources including the Soviet Union, and therefore, it can be argued, that the contribution of the Soviet Union to this process should not be overestimated. However, the crucial step in this process was taken in February 1970 when the Soviet Union formally agreed to associate the CEDB *rather than Dasturco* with the consultancy requirements of the continuous expansion of Bokaro to 4 million tonnes.

(2) The HSCL was incorporated on June 23, 1967 as a wholly-owned Government company for the purpose of undertaking the construction work on Bokaro. It was reported to consist mainly of over 300 engineers and technicians who had acquired construction experience in managing the civil engineering jobs at the Bhilai Steel Plant and the Heavy Electrical Plant at Bhopal. (For more details, see the *Hindu* [Madras], December 26, 1968.) On August 3, 1966, the Bokaro Steel Ltd. awarded to HSCL the civil engineering services of Dasturco. The revised contract with Dasturco was signed later on in January 1967.

DATE DUE